Praise
The Candle and t

CW01431921

"*Orion Foxwood holds the beacon of light at the dark crossroads where magic and mystery meet. I've been a guest at many of his workshops on conjure, folk magic and Witchcraft, and I'm delighted to see this book in print, sharing his knowledge and experiences. I'm sure, like me, you will find him simultaneously colorfully charismatic and deeply soulful, and soon, without realizing it, you and your magic will be changed for the better. That is the inspirational alchemy that Orion works on his students, readers and friends if you are open enough to listen, see and feel.*"

—CHRISTOPHER PENCZAK, founder of the Temple of Witchcraft and author of *The Plant Spirit Spirit Familiar*

"*There are places in the world where magic abounds, where its ancient practices stem from the very soul of the people living there. The Appalachian area of America is such a place. Much has been written about it, little is really known and even less is understood. Here is the real thing, half autobiography and half training manual with fascinating snippets of information thrown in. It is the genuine Appalachian belief system written by one born and bred to it. I have had the joy of Orion's friendship for many years and have worked with him on many occasions. Here in his own words you will find the result of his early training. He says clearly that this is a 'Way of Life'—one that if care is not taken will disappear and leave the world darker for its going. It is hard to give you more than just the barest flavor of the book here. Ancient practices still known and used today, information on herbs and spirit roads all written down by the loving hand of family memory. A gem to be treasured. Read it and you will be amazed at the richness that still exists in the heart of the Appalachians."*

—DOLORES ASHCROFT-NOWICKI, director of Studies
Servants of the Light

"Richly garnished with the knowledge and wisdom of personal experience, and offered in the conversational tone of a chat with an old friend, Orion Foxwood's The Candle and the Crossroads *serves the meat and potatoes of Southern Root Magic so deliciously, you'll savor every morsel—and anxiously await a second helping!"*

—DOROTHY MORRISON, author of *Utterly Wicked*

*"*The Candle and the Crossroads *is a unique book. It offers us an insight into the world of Appalachian Conjure that provides not only techniques and practices, but also a cultural context for those practices. Orion Foxwood's account of his life, and how he came by the knowledge and wisdom he shares, is every bit as important and informative as the techniques themselves. This book is one where the whole is much greater than the sum of its parts, laying bare as it does the heart and*

soul of Southern Conjure. There is no doubt in my mind that Orion is sharing with us a great treasure, and that he is part and parcel of that treasure. Practitioners of all traditions can learn much from this book, whether it be the nuts and bolts of technique, or through comparison with their own path. I will certainly be recommending this book to my own students of the Crooked Path."

—PETER PADDON, author of *A Grimoire for Modern Cunningfolk, Visceral Magick and Enchantment: The Witch's Art of Manipulation through Gesture, Gaze and Glamour*

"Orion is the most eloquent magical teacher of our time and proves it with The Candle and the Crossroads. You are immersed in Orion's teachings and come away enlightened and ready to doctor the root of your own self."

—JACKI SMITH, author of *Coventry Magic* and founder of Coventry Creations

"Orion writes from the heart. The Candle and the Crossroads is a very soulful book. He gives you a clear vision of the oral tradition from the Appalachian Mountains. I found his book very refreshing and I enjoyed reading it."

—STARR CASAS, rootworker and founder of *www .oldstyleconjure.com*

"The Candle and the Crossroads is a fascinating adventure into the spiritual path and work of Conjure as seen through the eyes of one of its modern practitioners, a soulful teacher of great depth and wisdom. Drawing on many years of experience, Orion Foxwood offers *the reader practical and powerful tools of blessing and transformation that have universal application while still being grounded in an original American path. This book is a crossroads itself, inviting you to connect with one of America's own root spiritual traditions."*

—DAVID SPANGLER, author of *The Laws of Manifestation, Apprenticed to Spirit,* and *Subtle Worlds: An Explorer's Field Notes*

"Like Witchcraft, conjure is the magic of the people, that wisdom and power hidden within us all that is accessible to everyone regardless of economic status, and, like Witches, conjurers and rootworkers embrace this power as a vocation to help those in need. It works within the context of all religions for it is the spirit that flows through them all. Orion Foxwood imparts centuries of folk wisdom from Appalachian, African, and other sources in this powerful compendium of knowledge that will help you to transform your life and the lives of others."

—CHRISTIAN DAY, author of *The Witches' Book of the Dead*

The
CANDLE
and the
CROSSROADS

The
CANDLE
and the
CROSSROADS

A Book of Appalachian Conjure and Southern Root Work

ORION FOXWOOD

WEISERBOOKS
San Francisco, CA / Newburyport, MA

First published in 2012 by Weiser Books
Red Wheel/Weiser, LLC

With offices at:
665 Third Street, Suite 400
San Francisco, CA 94107
www.redwheelweiser.com

ISBN: 978-1-57863-508-5

Library of Congress Cataloging-in-Publication Data available upon request

Cover design by Jim Warnèr
Cover photograph © Cusp / SuperStock
Interior by Maureen Forys, Happenstance Type-O-Rama
Typeset in Warnock Pro with Frutiger and Linoscript

Printed in the United States of America
MAL

10 9 8 7 6 5 4 3 2 1

The paper used in this publication meets the minimum requirements of the
American National Standard for Information Sciences—Permanence of Paper
for Printed Library Materials Z39.48-1992 (R1997).

There is an age-old, soulful calling that comes through our spirit from the voice of magic. This voice is older than time, and it comes from a very deep place in our spirit and the ancestral echoes that flow like a river in our blood—a stream as old as the human species. It rises from an ancient place of memory; it can never be silenced or hushed. The callings of this voice rise inside us and speak prayers of spirit; names of power; and directives of vision when the storms of the human world rage the most. This voice becomes louder and stronger when it is most needed, when our freedom to live and prosper is challenged. This voice summons us to reach to our spirit, the Spirit, and the spirit world for unseen hands to tip the forces of life toward wellbeing of mind, soul, body, and spirit. Conjure is one such voice!

Conjure and root work have endured the horrors of slavery, the challenges of poverty, and the forces of racism and inequality. They have held in trust the unbreakable core of human spirit. The early ancestors of conjure and root work may have perished in body, but they have endured in spirit. It is the flame of their powerful spirit that passes to each true conjure and root worker. This spirit flame passes into the candles each of us light to gather the blessings of the spirit world and God to our lives. When earnestly called at the crossroads of life or at the intersection of the seen and unseen spirit world, this spirit will greet us, impossible and miraculous.

To "Ole-Maker," the helpful spirits, the ancestors of conjure, and to those persons who seek to doctor the root and conjure the spirit in a sacred way that is worthy and honoring of the blood, sweat, and tears of those who preserved these ways.

Contents

Preface

I was born in 1963 with the "veil" (a localized term for the second sight) in the Shenandoah Valley in Virginia, an area that is rich in folklore, folktales, ghost stories, folk healing, and magic. Over the course of my life there and my travels in the American South, I was exposed to practices of Appalachian spirituality, second sight traditions, folk magic, and conjure. I also became familiar with southern and African-American root-doctoring traditions. Aspects of these are covered throughout this book. This is the source of my teachings and techniques.

Other than a few very brief quotes, the stories, spiritual and magical practices, and the folk wisdom in this book have been distilled from oral traditions in my family, culture, and subsequent sharing with other conjure workers. Some material also came directly through the guidance of God (the Source) and the spirits, the truest of teachers. What I have shared with you is from the traditions and practices of those who taught me conjure, spirit work, and root-doctoring specifically from the American southern and Appalachian oral traditions. They do not represent a universal or orthodox practice, as there is *no such thing* in the American South. This practice changes from geographic location to location, family to family, and sometimes even among ethnic groups. In brief, I offer to you the "soulful magic" of living tradition!

Acknowledgments

This book has been years in the making, and there are many beings—human (in and out of bodies) and other—who have contributed to me as a conjureman and to the life and teachings in this book. Thank you, and may all of the good spirits of life bless you with the seeking of your spirit.

I dedicate this book to:

God, Great Spirit, and the countless names for the Source, for you are everything about everything that I am and do. "May I see me the way you saw me when you made me."

My blood mother Betty Jean and my sister Donna Gale for the gift of the veil and the courage to use it. There would be no me without you!

My beautiful beloved one, Aubrey Taylor-Smith, for endless love and support—your very birth is a blessing to my world!

Ms. Granny and Johnnie Rooster, the first spirits to guide me to conjure. You opened the door that has opened doors for so many others.

Marie Laveau, the nineteenth-century Queen of New Orleans Voodoo, for being an example of the power of conjure in the face of racial adversity. My altar lights burn for you!

My dear best friend, Jhim Midgett, for a list of things too long to mention.

Priestess Miriam Chamani, Queen Mother of the Voodoo Spiritual Temple in New Orleans, for the many years of love, friendship, and rich spiritual wisdom you have shared with me.

Bloody Mary, New Orleans Voodoo Queen, for your love, friendship, integrity, and outstanding guidance in the conjure and Voodoo practices of New Orleans.

My publisher family, Weiser Books, for the voice of spirit you are to the world. My amazing editors: Amber Guetebier and Marienne Hartwood.

My beloved friend Lady Ceres Moon Spinners, for your boundless love and wisdom.

My conjure-crossroads family: Momma Starr Casas, Susan Diamond, Auntie Sindy Todo, and Shimmering-Wolf for your love, wisdom, guidance, and friendship on the path of hoodoo, conjure, and root doctoring.

Cat Yronwode for your trailblazing work on hoodoo and conjure. I honor you!

Joseph, Michelle, Sophie, and doggy-Graymond for your love, support, and the sanctuary of your home while I was writing this book.

To the spirit of Coco Robicheaux, New Orleans conjureman and blues musician extraordinaire, for the opportunity to meet and become a friend to you just before you passed into spirit. You reminded us that each precious moment we share together is a gift from God!

To the conjurers who had the power and courage to prevail and give us all the wisdom of their lives. Your spiritual power guides us all through the veil of forgetfulness into the light of spiritual awakening!

Chapter 1

Magic and Spirit Sight in My Folk Culture and Personal Work: A View from Within

There is a field where matter, mind, and magic meet. Meet me there and let's make the magic that made the world.

—ORION FOXWOOD AND BRIGH

This invocation came through me during a session of turning my awareness inward toward the eternal stream of ancestral presence, essence, and universal rhythm that knows no end and is always beginning. Many cultures call this technique meditation. My mother called it "the knowing." It is into this state of being that all conjurers go for inspiration, incarnation, evocation, and invocation. It dwells where the web of fate and the river of stars join in a dance of creation and revelation. To engage in these states of being, magic workers must part the perceived veil between the worlds and take the spirit of their seeking to that place where humanity and divinity meet—the crossroads. At the crossroads, the gate to the web of fate opens and the spirit roads are available. The mouth of creation opens to the mill of stars and magic is made manifest. Place your feet firmly on the existence of your life in this world, for that is the magical dance floor. Reclaim your presence in this world as the head of the great serpentine path of magic. Its vertebrae are the steps you have walked before that lead you into this world at this time. Its winding ways draw the worlds into one egg. Join me on a walk from my first home to building the home within that knows no bounds—the journey to my spirit and into the spirit world. If the path of the conjurer calls to you, this will be a good crystal ball for viewing the path to walking in the spirit land. This book is about spirit work, spiritual wisdom, love and power, and direct partnership with healthy spirit forces. *It is about bearing the candle flame of our inner spirit to the crossroads of transition and realignment with the very forces that are our source.*

The Journey to My Spirit

When I moved from my family home and southern culture in the Shenandoah Valley of Virginia to Maryland in the 1980s, I was on a quest for more people like me. I sought freedom to be out of the closet as a gay man and a magic worker, and more access to teachers and information on magical practices. I was beginning my voyage into the discovery of myself on many levels—a common theme for a young man, especially one (as my mom would say) who was "so damn different." I had no idea what it would take for me to become what my spirit had chosen for this life walk. In retrospect, it is good that spirits born as humans (such as you and I) who are marked to be magic workers do not know the fine print and the implications of a life devoted to magic. I think that if we did, we would surely run for the metaphorical hills and hide beneath a cloth of mediocrity.

The spirits that work with us are generous to shelter our direct perception from the details of the work we are called to do until life has carved out of us the ability to receive it, the inner clarity to see it, and the skills to implement it. One thing I know is that if you came into your body at birth marked for magic, there is no way around it. You must not betray your spirit's voice and turn away from what I have found to be a life of meaning and miracles. Dear reader, walk with me through a century or so of pages into old magic, deep spirit, wise ways, and paths of recovery, discovery, and sorcery that work with and from the source and center. If what you read speaks to what your spirit knows, then may those good spirits who sit above you guide you on this journey into the root of all things—the living spirit. May the wise ancestors place your feet in right relationship with the directive of your spirit. *And may you know when to make magic and when to let magic make you.*

The Baby Steps

The kind of beginning described herein is the most important first step for anyone who plans to walk the shadow roads that lead in and out of the world of forms, forces, shapes, and shapers. It is a journey to recover one's own spirit. The spirit within is the interface point between all forms of life—seen and unseen—and spirit pathways. My journey began as all true roads to the soul do: away from the familiar track of the voices outside to a recovery of the knowing voice within—the one that inspired my birth. But first comes the tuning in to what we, without external contaminations, feel and sense about our core. Then comes the unbinding of illusions, fears, and consensus reality to make room for the re-weaving of self from the core of spirit. Indeed, it all started like the Fool card in the tarot—by stepping off the cliff of the familiar past onto a vague cloud of inner guidance and into a new and foreign land of opportunity and challenge.

In order to know the spirit world, you must first know and manage your spirit—a task more challenging than it may sound. Magic is about doctoring the root of our self, making spirit relationships and thereby getting into creation's magical mix as a worker in the field of spirit that feeds and sustains all life. Did I mention that root workers and conjurers are nosy by nature? We want to know how life operates. We are not satisfied to sit on the sidelines. We get in the kitchen when life is being cooked up. These forms of magic are about power. Healthy power in this context is about our ability to create our lives in partnership with the web of life. Magic is about the freedom of the spirit to grow healthily without the tyranny of outside forces attempting to silence its inner voice.

Stepping Out onto the Cloud

Like Moses in search of the Promised Land, I just knew that the big city offered me promise. It gave me options to reveal the pulse driving outward from within and a sort of invisibility cloak under which I could be me in all my unfolding facets. Indeed, it exposed me to teachers in the magical arts and opportunities for uniqueness to blossom. In the course of that great adventure, I have studied and/or been initiated into Wiccan and Traditional Witchcraft lineages and New Orleans Voodoo practices, worked with Western Mystery practices, refined and deepened my Faery work, and expanded my conjure repertoire. I was on a search for truth that led me to new paths, such as witchcraft, and deeper into the magic of my cultural roots, conjure. Little did I know that ultimately magic starts from knowing the deep, abiding voice from within.

In many ways I felt like Dorothy in the classic film *The Wizard of Oz*—the thing I truly longed for most was home. And, like Dorothy, the power to get there was with (or in) me all along. What I did not understand was that home is an inside job. I was blessed to encounter and be taught by teachers who understood magic, spirituality, and mystical work. They knew the necessary elements of developing a "natural conjurer" (a person with blood-born spirit talents) and the skills needed for encountering and working in the spirit world in ways that leverage very potent effects. This is not to say that they were always loving, kind, or ethical. They were gifted . . . and they were human! I also did not realize what I already had within me from my cultural and familial magical practices. Sometimes we have to go away from ourselves to find ourselves. Without reservation, that is exactly how I came into the potency of my witchery and conjure.

My road to discovering my spiritual, mystical, and magical path has been one of revelation, retrieval, and integration. It has been a path of deep in-looking, sometimes earth-shattering change, and exchange with spirit beings in ways that left me permanently woven into the in-scape of our world and poised at the crossroads where human and other encounter, exchange, and reveal wisdoms only known by those brave enough to walk between paths of light and shadow. This book will present some of my discoveries on the path of conjure (or spirit work, as it was called in my culture) as well as some practical insights, techniques, and practices.

The Foundations of My Magic

My work in the spirit world originated through my mother and sister as well as the culture in the foothills of Appalachia in West Virginia and outside of Winchester, Virginia. I was born with the veil, a subject I will discuss in later chapters. Over the course of my life in Appalachia, I was exposed to the practices of my mother, neighbors, and other people in the family and community who had many of the following gifts or skills:

- **Spirit sight:** The ability to perceive invisible beings and the spirit-paths

- **Working by the signs:** The ability to synchronize work such as farming, fertility of humans and animals, orcharding, and more with the influence of the zodiacal influences; or to interpret tokens or communication from the unseen spirit world also known as signs

- **Conjuring with spirits:** The ability to pray or otherwise call to otherworld beings such as God, angels, ancestral spirits, local nature spirits, crossroads beings, etc., for doing magical work

- **Faith healing:** The ability to induce physical, emotional, mental, or spiritual healing through direct contact and mediation of divine healing power

- **Setting magical lights (candle magic):** The ability to use fire in candles (especially), hearth fires, and other flames to set spiritual light to petitions or prayers

- **Doctoring the root:** The ability to use herbs, roots, stones, or animal parts (bones, claws, fur, etc.) for magic or the clearing, cleansing, and blessing of the spirit of a person (also known as his or her root)

- **Praying and/or dreaming true:** The ability to bring the successful blessings of spirit/God to a person, place, or thing, as well as predictive or informative dreaming

- **Blessing or cursing:** The ability to bring spirit influences (helpful or harmful) to a situation or desire through any of the aforementioned abilities

In this book, I will discuss and share some techniques for honing these abilities and others.

All of the magical practices in my family and community were practical and tied to everyday life. The worker was both feared and revered. He or she was often consulted when all other interventions failed; the services were purchased under the cloak of night. These practices were not and are not a counter-culture, hobby, or spiritual path. They are a vocation, practice, and a paradigm, and have a definite role in society. Understanding this is important to comprehending the philosophical underpinnings of this book. The roots of my conjure are African slave and other ethnic practices mixed in with Christian belief, Native American practices, European Witchcraft, and Faery beliefs—and I am sure there are other elements that I have not identified.

Why This Book?

The fuel for writing this book was my concern that people who are, as my partner Aubrey calls it, "magically inclined," read a lot but too often do very little in the way of applying the practice of magic, spirituality, and mysticism to improving the quality of their lives. In my experience, magic has too often become an intellectual pursuit to the exclusion of actual skills development and betterment of everyday life. This approach leaves the worker feeling filled with facts but void of fulfillment. My mother always said, "In the end, when we take our last breath in this life, it is likely that we will want to know if we were loved, if we loved, and if we were happy." These practices should enhance the pursuit of life, liberty, and happiness—that includes inner peace, joy, prosperity, health, and a host of other blessings. These streams of spirit development, spirituality, mysticism, and magic are enlivened by living. You cannot think your way into magical potency, spiritual knowing, and mystical union. You have to consistently work the magic in order to have an established relationship with its workings.

Like so many who walk the magic roads, I have accumulated stacks of books, tons of crystals, temples full of statues, and enough herbs and oils to choke a dinosaur. Too often we look everywhere but in our country and family for solid magical practices. Yet this country is rich in magical lore, techniques, and practices. These practices are overlooked because they are too familiar or close, or they are seen as superstitious and not evolved. This last statement is inaccurate; folk magic is the mother of temple magic and formalized religion.

Ask yourself: is it wise to cast away the root of a plant for the use of its fruits? The fruits live for a season, but the roots live through the seasons. This book looks at the deep-rooted magic of the common folk. With that said, all of us are (to some degree) on a path to self-discovery, life fulfillment, and wholeness. As I have continued to grow in conjure, I have discovered that the cord that weaves wholeness of spirit is best woven with three threads: spirituality, mysticism, and magic. I will go deeper into these threads in the next chapter. Seeking magical work without spiritual development and mystical practices is dangerous because it lacks moral fiber, visionary guidance, wisdom, and a sound understanding of the shadowy and light forces at work within you. This book will discuss lore, beliefs, practices, and techniques for witchcraft and conjure rooted in these three threads and poised on a foundation of practicality and applicability.

This book is about the conjure way of life, its soul, and to the depth of what my friend Starr Cassis calls "Old Style Conjure." My old-style conjure works with the Bible, the crossroads, spirits, stones, roots, baths, rivers, trees (living and dead), laying on of hands, sin-eating, prayer clothes, altars, setting lights (candles or lamps), and a host of other materials. It works with cloth from a workman's shirt, coal from deep mines, thread from feed and seed bags, honey and liquor, and other materials found in everyday life. My conjure works with real power placed in everything by spirit. It does not visualize. It knows! God (or the Maker) is not distant—it is close and has spirits sent to us to help us. My conjure was taught to me by old people, poor people, spirited people, and families who trusted me and let me in on their cherished knowledge.

Magic as a Path to Freedom

For years, I have pondered the role of magic in the development of spirit in the human quest for knowing. Ultimately, spirituality, mysticism, and magic are approaches to relating one's own spirit to the spirit of all life. As I have looked deeper into the practical and occult roles of magic, I have found that magic appears to be a partner with the nature of spiritual freedom, which I define as the right to hear the voice of our own spirit and to create a life that is satisfying and meaningful in a cultural and planetary context. Magic liberates the seeker from being force-fed a diet of adherence and allows him or her to directly engage, encounter, and exchange with the forces of creation and life from the inside in an aware and co-creative manner.

Magic makes its face known where emotional, physical, or spiritual oppression attempts to chain the spirit of humanity. Consider the legendary roles of magic in the exodus of the Jewish tribes from Egypt (i.e., the parting of the sea, turning a staff into a serpent, and so on), the use of Voodoo in the Haitian slave revolt of 1791, or the mythic slave revolt of the Italian people led by Aradia through her Dianic Witchcraft. Whether magic played a role in these events—or whether they even occurred at all—is not the point. The fact remains that magic appears in urban myths, mythic battles, fights against oppression, or rebuttal against enforced norms.

Magic is a fire that destroys the fetters that bind the spirit. It is a gift to life and humanity that allows us to consciously shape our lives through direct engagement with the spirit inside life and inside ourselves. I believe that magic, specifically the magical practices of the common folk, has always been and always will be associated with human freedom and the quest for a good life.

It All Began with the Veil

I was born in Winchester, Virginia, in 1963. Southern and Appalachian folk culture and beliefs were still very much a part of the ways of the poor folk—my folk. I have often semi-jokingly said that we were "po-people" because we could not afford the other "o-r" in the word *poor*. My mother lived by her inner-knowing, as did her mother and many of the male elders in the family and community. She consulted God on everything, or as she would say, "I take my spirit to the throne for heavenly direction." She was born with what we call the veil—a placental sheath over the face of the baby indicating that they have the blessing. The blessing is the ability to see into the world of the spirit, and it shows up in different ways for each person. Today, one might think of the blessing, and its resulting gift called the knowing, as extrasensory perception (ESP), though we would have never used such a big term. It is no surprise that I was born with the veil, too, as was my beautiful sister, Donna.

My culture had mixed feelings about the veil. To some, it was seen as a blessing and a call to the pulpit to be a preacher of God's word. For others, it was seen as a curse to be avoided because no good could come of it. In fact, my mom said that when she asked to see me after the birth, the nurses said I was okay, but "different." They said I was born with white hair, pointed ears, and the veil—and they already had a preacher ready to pray the devil out of me. This was the equivalent to a form of exorcism. My mother was furious at their audacity and checked out early from the hospital. Needless to say, the exorcism failed.

My blessing began to open at the age of seven. This opening was premature; it happened when I was visited by the ghost of my grandfather. He came to me gasping for air and hanging from a rope. I was terrified. I screamed, and my father grew angry, telling me to stop seeking attention and go to sleep. Finally, my mother said, "Ernie, it's happening. His veil is lifting." My mother took me to my grandfather's house to attempt to settle me. Sadly, there he was, swinging from a rope in his barn. Publicly, there is still conjecture about whether he committed suicide or was murdered. Privately, we all knew he had been lynched because he loved a woman "from the otha side of the tracks." With this token (spirit contact or sign), my life in the spirit world had begun, and there was no turning back.

As the years rolled along, my tokens expanded from spirits of the dead to local nature spirits, God, Jesus, angels, the man at the crossroads, and a host of otherworld beings (or as we called them, "side-winders"). I met snake handlers, faith healers, root doctors, sin-eaters, and other spirited people. Most of these workers considered themselves to be fine and upstanding Christian people. I loved going to church, and occasionally Jesus would show up. I often got in trouble for seeing him and asking about his mom. I even preached for a while as a youth minister and sang in a gospel trio (Goddess forbid) at local hymn sings. These are events where gospel singing groups visit churches in worship and praise. They conclude with a big picnic or a blessing in the graveyard on Decoration Day (aka Memorial Day Sunday). With all this said, there were troubles in my spirit and they were driving me out of the church.

If we are built in God's image, why is his mother not discussed? Why are supposedly loving people so restrictive with God's love? If we can be like Jesus, then why aren't there more miracles performed? If the Psalms came from God's word (the Bible) and some folks worked them in magic for a good life, then why was this being called the devil's work? Why do I feel God's presence more in nature than in a church? How can little babies be born sinful when they are precious and innocent? Why does God hate gay people for loving their partners when God is love? Why are women, from whence all babies come, treated with such disrespect? Why do I have to wait for death to meet God and Jesus directly when I see and talk to them all the time? Why can't a preacher teach me how to use my veil to serve God's work? Why did preachers I know talk bad about the faith healing and two-headed preachers (who work with the spirits and angels, etc.) when they helped people in very real ways?

I found that the folks who practiced spirit work were helping people in measurable ways. It was restoring an experienced and informed faith that was often broken by blind faith and preachers who had no experience of a living God. Don't get me wrong—many of these preachers were good people of faith, but they were without direct and tangible experience with God and his/her power. It seemed to me that one cannot bring God's power and presence to the people unless he or she is living in it. My blasphemous curiosity and concerns for life and people (alive and dead), and my desire to be an agent for God's will and spirit, caused me to knock on other doors. First, I looked at my feelings without the direction of other humans. I delved deeper into the "Mother Spirit" I felt when I was alone with nature. I went to the crossroads at night to meet the Dark Rider—a spirit that opens the spirit roads. I stopped waiting for the spirit world to find me. I sought it out, and find it I did . . . in its beauty and horror. But then, none of us learned how to walk without falling down.

The Role and Feel of Magic in My Folk Culture

We are in the midst of a wonderful revival of magical and mystical interest that started in the 1800s and continues to solidify the bridges between the worlds. Incredible movements and magical systems continue to enlighten us, such as the Golden Dawn, theosophy, spiritualism, Thelema, Wicca, and the New Age movement—the list goes on. These systems bring invaluable resources; however, there was magical bedrock already here, and too often I feel that that foundation is trivialized or forgotten. This bedrock is the folk magical practices. There are hundreds of streams of folk magic, but in this book I will only address the ones I have been shaped by in hopes that they will inspire you to look deeper. The folk ways re-sacredize our everyday life and place the spirit world right here . . . right now . . . as close as your breath.

The conjure practices I grew up with and continue to practice are practical. They deal with all levels of life—spirituality, love, material prosperity, justice, health, happiness, attractiveness, fertility, and management of your life and its spirit in all directions. It is not a religion. It is not a political expression. It is not a counterculture. It is a lifestyle. It is a skill, a craft, and an art form. It is respected as a form of doctoring, though it is not a medical practice. It is focused on doctoring your spirit and its relationship to the creator, ancestors, the good spirits, and forces one may see as luck or wellbeing. It can be used to harm someone, though I do not recommend this. It has centuries of results behind it, and myriad techniques and recipes within it. The role of the magic worker is counselor, advisor, luck bringer, healer of the spirit, and last chance for wholeness when no one else can help. The roles of the conjurer are congruent with the practices of the old style witches who I also met and learned from. Therefore, it is nearly impossible for me to give a solid introduction to my conjure world without giving some brief information on my development as a witch as well.

Encountering Family and Folk Witches

Around 1980, I had my first encounters with what I call "old style" or "traditional" witches. They were a lovely older couple from Brentwood, Essex, England visiting their son in Winchester, Virginia. I was in my late teens, working as a busboy at a local restaurant. We met at the salad bar, which I was restocking. They did not wear any magical jewelry or look different from any other older people, so magic was not the first item in our chats—it was their request for more croutons. At that time, I was a backwoods boy with very little traveling under my young belt, so exotic English accents and life in a foreign land fascinated me. I mentioned root work and the crossroads. They said they did something similar in their family.

We became friends, and the couple visited their son many times over the two and a half years that we knew each other. This opened discussions on what they called turnings (spells), the little people (Faery beings), the magic mill (a form of magic working the power of the earth), bad-washers (people who did harmful magic), overlooking (the evil eye), and a host of other simple but potent practices. They told me that witchcraft is what some of their family members called it, but they preferred "hedgery" and cunning. There were no initiations—just techniques and minor (but profound) lore.

I lost contact with them when I moved to Maryland. My spirit says they have long since died, as they were easily in their mid-seventies when I met them.

Over the years since, I have met several family or folk witches. Consistently, I have found that their practices feel similar to the conjure practices of the South. They work with spirits of the dead, crossroads spirits, Faery beings, angels, and spells to affect our spirit and overall wellbeing. Both types of magic workers see spirits as living beings, independent of humanity. They see magic as flowing through both hands, meaning it can help or harm. However, both conjurers and witches have some of the most sound ethics I have seen. They tend to be direct in their concerns and potent in their convictions. A perfect example of this is my spirit grandmother in the old art of witchcraft, Lady Circe. She was a hereditary witch who incorporated Wiccan elements into her practices in the 1970s. Her magic and wisdom were direct and potent. She served the community on all levels, doing tarot for multiple generations, helping the homeless and the drug addicted, and often giving her last penny for the wellbeing of another person (human or animal).

Living a Life as a Spirit in a Spirited World

This chapter is an introduction into some of the practices (cultural and other) that have shaped the conjurer and witch that I am today. It is a mere introduction, because there is much more. Rather than continue with my experiences, I will share with you teachings, techniques, and workings in the chapters to come. I would be remiss if I did not bring your focus on a profound part of this work: *you and I are spirits in a human experience.* We are involved in a walk-through form, carrying our spirit and our ancestors to new experiences of healing, revelation, and understanding. We are bringing awareness to our consciousness and power to our presence with each step we take.

If you want to have a life that is deeply enriched and enriching by the paths I share in this book, then you have to engage life as a spirit in a spirit-filled world. Life neither begins nor ends with that which is experienced by our outer senses or perceivable by our current standards and instruments used in science. Our sciences may be able to approach the spirit world one day, but they must move from approaches that look through deduction and reduction. The spirit cannot be held outside of its connections to greater rhythms. It interpenetrates everything and is the source of our inspirations, thoughts, insights, feelings, behaviors, relationships, events, encounters, and every other experience that we can imagine. At every level of life is aliveness. In all states of aliveness is intelligence. In the spirit work, everything is a person except the original word and light that summoned forth life. It is beyond personages, but lives through them. The spirit world is teeming with life, and we are all a part of it. If you experience that now, while in form, then death loses its existence. As a conjurer and a witch, you walk with the spirits as one of them. Welcome to your true home! Welcome to walking the shadow roads of spirit!

Chapter 2

The Three Paths to Cultivating the Spirit

Three roads to one will lead to the sun.
—Orion Foxwood and Johnnie Rooster

As I have worked with, and been worked by, magical and spirit forces, it has become abundantly clear that most people know more about others (or at least how they appear) than they know about themselves. If they have journeyed the landscape of self, it has usually been in the realms of the mind, body, and behavior but very little in the wholeness that connects them to the abiding spirit. Yet our own spirit is the creating and meeting place of a great web of creation, and it is our most important spirit ally. It is the gateway to the whole spirit world, including the creator itself, and it fits us like a perfectly formed keyhole with our personality as the key. In short, it is our truest nature and the place of creation for our human nature. To retrieve our alignment with it, we must look inward to the mystery of our own essential essence, our aliveness, and then reflect outward on how we do or do not create in congruence with it. This essence is our true root of being.

Too often, and to our own detriment, inward looking beyond psychological and emotional forces to the energetic and soul-level terrain is like entering uncharted and forbidden frontiers. In fact, we are often told to either stay focused on the "real" world outside or to avoid a personal dialogue with our spirit beyond specific religious rules. This cultural malady is the beginning of what I call "the spell of forgetfulness," a concept I will address in more detail throughout this book. There are subtle forces and tides of spirit moving through our inner feelings, mental dialogue, and body senses all the time; they are the shapers of our interaction with the world of form. At the feeling levels, these form our soul—a deep well of wisdom, mystical union, and magical potency.

The mental images that run through our head shape the power that flows from our spirit and its interactive soul, and our response to them defines so much of our image of ourselves, our world, and our place in that world. Sadly, our mainstream culture teaches us that the composition of our own secret rhythms is the one place we dare not go, for surely there must be menacing demons waiting there. If there are, they likely originate in the human fear of "God," nature's Garden of Eden, and our fated role in the spirit and vision of our world.

I am here to say that is not only false—it is the deadliest lie ever fed to us. A powerful quote from the Gospel of Thomas speaks clearly about this: "If you bring forth that which you have within you, it will save you. If you do not, it will destroy you" (Saying 70). Becoming conscious to our aliveness—aware in our spirit, and sovereign over it—is what matters most in our lives. Knowing, healing, and growing our spirit is the most important thing we must do in our embodiment on earth. Contacting and clearing the shadow forces that bar the sacred entry to the wonderment of our soul and the power of our spirit is crucial to both find joy and discover an inner platform for contacting and leveraging the powers of other spirit beings, the living well of the Mother Spirit, and the potent forces awaiting revelation in our own spirit. As my mother always said, "Claim your spirit or someone or something else will!"

I have never received better counsel than this. But, the soul and spirit's language require us to enter into a constant, committed, and consistent dialogue. Our intellect and reason is of no substantial use to us in this area of our lives. In fact, our intellect is the servant, not the master, to our spirit. Until our thinking is inspirited and cleansed, we risk running powerful spirit voltage through faulty and fragile wiring, thus inducing an energetic house fire. Before working with other spirits, be they embodied, disembodied (ancestral), or never embodied, the dialogue *must* begin with our most intimate spirit companion—*our own spirit.*

The first step in acquainting our consciousness with our spirit is understanding the elements of our lives that reflect, but do not compose, our spirit. These elements are all of the masks we use in the many ways we are reflected into the physical and social worlds. The mirror is the patterns and forms of your life and your reactions to it. Ask yourself: Am I enslaved by the forms of my life and the fears in my emotions? If so, it is time to clean out the spaces within you and the forms they take in your outer life. This will be addressed at length in the discussion on cleaning your shoes (spiritual cleansing).

Unfortunately, and in most cases, our response to the forces working within us is solely based on social roles, relationships, and expectations instead of deeper contemplation and contact with who and how we are in our core—our spirit. Too often, our uncontaminated feelings (meaning those without exterior influence) are muted at best, mutated at worst, and comprise the final frontier of our discoveries instead of the root of our revelations. This is the "forced silence of the spirit" that my mother spoke of when I was a child. I call this the spell of forgetfulness. Without the voice of our spirit, we are ships without sails and oars, mastered by an unlicensed and incompetent captain who has no map.

The well-schooled captain's voice is still within us, though the ship has been in the hands of strangers who parade around as the voice of our spirit. My mother called this voice "the knowin.'" She called the other voices "uninvited guests." The foundational work of the magic worker is to know the difference between the voice of the knowing and the voice of the uninvited and to organically dismiss the uninvited guests as the shadowy forces they are.

Many of these forces come into our spirit at a young age through crisis and trauma. The retrieval of our spirit is the most arduous, yet wonderful, of all the journeys. The full force of our spirit to the present, the only thing that is real, is the beginning of becoming a powerful spirit and magic worker. Breaking the shackles of our past and the domination of our fear-master gives us the power to be effective conjurers and root workers. If you are not willing to do this part of the work, then indeed magic is a dangerous road to travel, laden with harmful forces that ensnare you. These forces lie within, and they can be cured. Your root can be doctored. Know this: if you are always living in the past, then you are always dying and not living in the spirit.

Governance over our interior world is undervalued in our society. It is rarely given voice unless it contributes directly to our post-industrial world. If it cannot be observed as contributing to the workforce, family structure, or overall productivity, then it is a distraction from the real work of being a good and productive citizen. What about inner peace, joy, contentment, and other spirit qualities that require no external stimulus? These qualities grant power, sovereignty, and authority over one's spirit(s) and its external embodiment. They grant us the power to stand before the spirits as a potent spirit in our own right. It is interesting to note that it is rare that a family member is sent to a psychiatrist or therapist simply because he or she is unhappy. Rather, the individual usually comes to the threshold of healing because he or she is not functioning in a manner that is socially acceptable. They have lost touch with what is socially sanctioned and important, including such qualities as productivity or compliance. They are making folks around them uncomfortable. Well, conjure is not about making people comfortable. It is about making people powerful, whole, healthy, and happy. In combination, these states form an amazing individual. This individual is awaiting discovery and revelation inside each one of us.

The most primary task for any incarnate human is retrieving his or her inner-knowing. By using the term *primary*, I am suggesting that if there is one aim for any human being to make as his or her number one priority, it should be to concretize a consistent contact with the flow of his or her own life force. Our life force is the energetic quality that we share with everything in the embodied world of nature and the touchpoint between the seen and the unseen, the human and the divine. If honored and nurtured, it will tell us all that we need to know to navigate through our lives while in a body. It is the seat of our inner-knowing, often called intuition. This inner-knowing is connected to the voice of God or the essential core in everyone and everything. This core is also known as the soul, which is a personalized aspect of the eternal nature of spirit. It is the point where the web of spirit dips a thread from us into the world. Through it, the spirit worker's conjure comes. It is the special something that we all have, but it must be awakened from sleep, conjured out of the inner cave, and grown into this world.

There is a feeling of unity and aliveness that comes to us when we tap this level of our lives. For some, it is easier because of genetic propensities. In fact, for those of us born with the veil, the witch-blood, the faery-touch, or the hundreds of other related folk concepts, we often have no choice in its awakening. This can be unsettling in the absence of mentorship and guidance, and it's one of the reasons I have written this book. Too many of the elders who hold the folk wisdoms on developing the blessing are dying out. Folk magic cultures like my own are a dying breed. The world has too many self-proclaimed magic and spirit workers who have researched or transmitted information but possess no actual skills or wisdom. If a teacher has not been shaped by his or her work from the inside out, then he or she lacks the wisdom and power to work the spirit in healthy, balanced, and potent ways. These persons often scar true seekers and gifted students with self-doubt, broken faith, and wounds to the spirit. When gifted seekers are touched by well-taught spirit workers and/or witches, they will feel an innate understanding and aliveness in their spirit like nothing they have ever felt before. That state is where the conjurer lives, and it is the motivating force of their lives. It is the inspirited life of the spirit world. This is not to say that it is all rainbows and fun. No, there are challenges and shadow places of great terror. But it is better to die in truth than to live in lies. Spirit work is for the explorer of life.

The Invisible Threads to the Visible World

In the initial stages of spirit work, the student learns the flavor and language of his or her own soul and spirit. He or she learns how to discern me from not-me, healthy from toxic, true from untrue, and powerfully helpful from destructively deceptive. This reclamation of spirit is the single most important aspect of training in the world of the spirits. It is from this clear vantage point that the worker can engage, interact, and exchange with spirits and states of consciousness and perception at different levels of existence. However, I feel that it is useful to have some grounded knowledge of the states of spirits encountered in the soul's life to be able to discern one's soul's voice. There are states or neighborhoods in our inner world that should be mapped. They have resident powers and forces that must be acknowledged and understood for the worker to have sovereignty over his or her own spirit and to engage the spirit world from this point of awareness.

The examples of the states I am about to share are my family cultural concepts and do not represent an exhaustive list or a definitive cosmology for a broad culture. They are examples of one set of country lore in a folk practice. In short, they are from my "hillbilly magic." I have given both the folkloric cultural image and an explanation.

The Clearing

The first state is the clearing, which is the more obvious area for us who are in physical bodies. It seems clear to us (by and large) because it is where the bulk of our senses have been trained to look. It is a realm of seemingly clear distinctions, roles, and relationships. It is the world of appearances. Interestingly, spirits in nonphysical states say that our world is not as concrete as we think when seen from other-than-human eyes. In a healthy spirit life, there is a natural breathing between the realms (not a leaking). The worker helps his or her clients ensure that this state of energetic breathing is in place.

Like any clearing, it can also be a dumping ground for trash when left unmanaged. Anyone who has lived near woods has witnessed that there is a human tendency to dump trash just inside the woods. Back home we not-so-poetically call these "dumps." Spirit workers initially may have to clean off trash and reclaim their own life landscape. Lots of people share the clearing area with us, and they like to allegorically build on our property. So, the most reachable area is our physical world life, which Mom called the clearing.

The Paths into the Woods

The next state is called the paths into the woods (also known as footpaths). This is a transitional state that is liquid and sticky in energetic quality. It is the last state outward into the physical realms and the first you encounter when moving inward. Sometimes it needs to be cleaned of soul debris to make it "walkable" and understandable. Ancestral dead move onto the paths while detangling and dis-entrenching themselves from the clearing world of form as they move inward. Haunts of different kinds may reside there until they move to a more refined or defined level of life. The spirit worker also walks paths in the woods to see but not directly engage with otherworld beings. These narrow paths can be what many people call hellish places of redemption. My experience is that the content of our imagination will define what this world looks like when we transition (die) from the clearing to the woods.

The Deep Woods

The next state is the deep woods, which may seem to us physical folks as a subtle and inner state. It is an older level of life teeming with a spirit ecosystem. A part of us is always alive there; it is a strengthening place for the discarnate soul. It also is the soulful place of regeneration and deep wisdom. It has ancient trees, wisdom stones, and other place-states that are useful in our spirit's growth (or as I call it, in-scape). It is in this place within our soul that we can find deep wisdom and a river of life that connects us through all embodiments, minus the paradoxes and traumas of the individuated lifetime. Here, I refer to reincarnation or life in other states of existence as a component of my personal belief. Life in the spirit world before and after death is a part of my cultural beliefs; reincarnation is not.

As we approach it from our outer life, it may feel and appear as a hostile place guarded by frightening creatures and challenging feelings. However, these inner constructs are aspects of our own mindscapes—individually, culturally, and filially.

The Mountain of Vision

The next state is the mountain of vision (or song). This is a refined area where beings encounter what Mom would have called the voice of God on the mount. It is a state of being where vision is encountered and received—where heaven and the woods touch. This place within us is hallowed and holy. It is a transcendent state that moves our eyes heavenward from distraction into wholeness, vision, and power. In my practices, the worker seeks to be able to move into this state at will and to mind-touch or spirit-reach to forces that are powerful, clean, clear, and close to the source.

The Spirit Roads or Streams

The next state, the spirit roads or streams, is an area where life moves into and out of the spirit and embodied realms, bringing God's blessings/Mana, or life essence, to the world. Where the paths are consciousness-centered, the streams are primarily spirit-centered. Where the paths are for exploration inward and outward, the streams give sustenance and vital energy. Both the paths and the streams are important aspects of the worker's cultivation of active spirit growth and magic. The spirit worker will ride into and out of the other world through these breathing places, which may be drawn by a path that leads to a stream. They can also be places of cleansing and baptism. This is why we use creeks and rivers so much for our work. We also use wells and springs, but that is for reaching deep inner states of wisdom and memory. Through the streams and the deep wood, we may reach for the soul of the world and that place where our soul comes into its richest states of being.

Heaven

The next state is heaven, which was the source world. It is both the abode and the creator of the creator. It is, as my mother told me, "God's Momma." We do not go there until we are finished with life in the woods, paths, and clearings. However, the Maker (the first and creator spirit) sends blessings in the form of spirit and spirits from that place when prayed for or sent by grace. We can meet its grace and power on the mountains of vision through a technique we call praying true. In my work, grace is like space made within us by surrendering our fear and illusion of isolation for receiving the inflowing tide of living spirit. From the mountain of vision, the worker can reach to heaven as the Mother Spirit of creation, created and creating. All of the aforementioned states are sources of the worker's power and wisdom, depending on the need at hand.

❖ ❖ ❖

There is an unending list of beings that live in these states. Using a mix of folk concepts and language I have developed, here is a list of some of these beings:

- **Shadowy Spirits:** Non-conscious pictures of physical life seared into the environment, or parasitic emotional projections that seem to have a life of their own and feed on life force. They live in the edges of our being and are like dust-bunnies in the soul.

- **Haunts (also called Haints or Hants):** Spirit beings that may be well-meaning or not, healthy or unhealthy, and live close to the physical world. These include ghosts (human and other), nature spirits, guardian spirits, and other beings.

- **Holy Ancestors:** Ancestral human beings that are redeemed and spiritually whole and are considered wisdom keepers and mentors to the embodied humans. These beings are of immeasurable worth to the spirit worker. They may be called saints in many traditions. My mother always instructed me to bless all spirits that come with the "blood of Jesus" to ensure that they are holy. Clearly, this is a Christian form of blessing and consecration as well as purification and protection.

- **Helpers:** All kinds of beings that may help us, ranging from Faery to angelic and other spirits in between. In conjure, these spirits may be seen as members of a family with the worker. Other workers see them in a work-for-hire kind of relationship. Personally, I do not prefer this approach, as I think it is disrespectful and ultimately limits magical power.

- **Walker Spirits:** Spirits that move between all worlds. The conjurer and the spirits of song, fire, prayer rhythm, chants/charms, and other forms that bridge the meeting place of spirit are eventually Walker Spirits. These spirits move power across states of existence to and from the worker. Many workers I have known refer to the use of brooms, smoke, images of winged creatures, and other forms as Walker Spirits.

- **Soul Spirits:** All kinds of beings, including our own incarnating soul, that live in the soulful presence and memory of the earth and may include Holy Ancestors, deities of the earth and sea, animal and plant spirits, and Faery and other nature spirits.

- **The Maker(s):** Very powerful beings that are considered the creators of all worlds. In some traditions they are the

Goddesses, Gods, God, and Great Spirit. The Makers are powerful and holy and must be approached with humility and awe.

The greatest mystery of all this work is in understanding that there is an essence that connects all spirits and all states of being, which Mom called the voice/breath of God or the spirit tongue. Understanding this and the continuity of one's own essence through all times, states, and experiences brings the deepest levels of aliveness and spirit that passeth not.

Over years of doing this work, I have found that cultivation of our spirit is achieved through three approaches. In the course of using these three modes, workers will encounter other spirit beings that become a part of their family or their clearing work. I call these modes the three paths to cultivating the spirit. Many believe that the most powerful, potent, and healthy worker will have techniques, lore, traditions, and practices that relate to these paths regardless of religious beliefs or systems.

The Three Paths to Cultivating the Spirit

As I mentioned earlier, my mother, who is one of the wisest spirits I have ever known, often remarked, "Claim your spirit, or something or someone else will; nothing is ever wasted in this world." This was one of the clearest directives I have ever received from anyone about the number one priority of our existence. You see, the Maker planted a part of itself into all living things. This spark of eternal flame is the force that marshals our energetic composition, cell structures, mineral components, and genetic material into a design to bridge it into this awesome world of ours. It is a force so powerful that it pulled you from the un-manifest to the manifest, from an idea in the mind of God to a creation in the world of nature. However, trauma, thought-forms, illusion, and all of the other byproducts of the forces of forgetfulness can lead us from our spirit.

A great part of the reclamation of one's spirit is becoming conscious of what and who comes into your spirit and retrieving the preconditioned state of being. This state existed in you before you and I were even born. It is a seed of light always waiting to be grown into this world. Sadly, too many of us find it through sorrow and crisis, breaking our stronghold on a form of ourselves that must die so that our true spirit may live. But what if we knew our spirits more intimately and consistently? What if we knew how to consciously grow them into our world with a healthy and productive relationship to the forces of life? That should be a desire for all of us, and that is so much of what this work is about.

Over the many years I have been a seer, a witch, and a conjurer, I have noticed that there are three primary ways we can cultivate the divine potency within us into an expression in the physical world. After all, don't you think we were born to reveal that which is within us? The first steps are to find it, to own it, to heal it (with help from our spirits and Makers), and to grow it into the world and harvest the fruits of our own inspirited lives. The three paths to this work may be achieved in one life, but it often takes many lives. I mention many lives because I know that reincarnation is real; it is important to understand that from the level of our own spirit there is only *one* life with many states or embodiments. Once we understand that our "lives" are conditions of one life, we begin to heal that off/on approach to living that traumatizes our achievement of meaning and joy.

The three paths to cultivating the spirit are spiritual, mystical, and magical. These paths allow a dialogue and flow of life through our source-ful spirit, soulful center, and resourceful substance (physical form and life). This dialogue makes for a whole person. My personal working definitions of these three approaches to growing one's spirit are as follows.

The Spiritual Path

The spiritual path is an awareness that there is a spirit, force, or state of being of which all beings and states of existence are composed. It is omnipotent (all-powerful), omniscient (all-knowing), and omnipresent (everywhere). Most spiritual practices are centered on ways for understanding and appeasing the spiritual path with devotional practices and an aim toward a better afterlife. Sadly, there is too much mythology implying that this being is all-judging and full of oppressive righteousness, which leads to fear-based instead of love-based traditions. Too often, awe gets confused with fear, and fear creates separation illusions within and between us. Spirituality, in this practice, involves the cultivation of conscious living in the presence of an eternal sublime presence. As this path grows within us, so does conscious presence, compassionate love, unity, connectedness, and a host of other attributes. Fear, condemnation, self-absorption, callous actions, broad generalizations (such as racism, gender oppression, homophobia, humano-centrism, etc.), and other traits indicate a lack of spiritual awareness and work in this area. The spiritual path is the first step on the cultivation of the spirit.

The Mystical Path

The mystical path is an awareness that the spirit that made all things is also in all things. Therefore, the mystic will seek to understand the living presence of the one spirit (the Maker) within himself or herself and live a life in accordance with the spark of the living flame that lives within him or her. This spark may be seen as an individual's soul or an individualized stream of spirit moving through form. Mysticism, in this practice, involves the cultivation of conscious living from the presence of the Maker within us, embodied in the principle we call soul. This soul is the central axis of our existence and is the purpose we were issued from the ocean of being. The mystic has a sense of vision, even when clarity is muddled. The mystic sees the unifying power in all things and beings even when the expressions from that being are harmful, pain-driven, or fear-driven. This sense of personal meaning often leads the mystic into a healthy possession of his or her own spirit and the sacred responsibility to grow it. The mystic path is visionary, creative, self-reflective, inspired, and aware, and it always produces agents of change—subtly or overtly, depending on the calling of the mystic. The mystic path is a more advanced stage in the cultivation of the spirit.

The Magical Path

The magical path is an awareness of the Maker's means of making (to the level that we are able to understand such a holy and whole state). It is the art of conscious creation, in opposition to a constant action/reaction approach to creation, which leaves us only partly aware of why we do what we do. The magical path puts us in a co-creative relationship with the creation process and the forces at work in its mechanics. Magic allows us to be actively creating in the substance world. However, it is a touchy area rife with areas where our darker and more shadowy areas can wreak havoc until stopped by the mechanisms of the magical pool that draws all things back to its source. This book recommends magical practices that are ethical and soundly grounded through spiritual and mystical practices; otherwise you can find yourself in the clutches of your own shadow forces, creating a life of pain. A solid magic worker is a spirit worker first and a mystic first. Sound magic work, in my opinion, is the most advanced path in the growth of the spirit. This is why it is ill advised for anyone to engage in broad-scale, high-voltage magic until the spiritual and mystic work is solidly in place. I am not talking about the simple magic of getting a better job, cleansing and clearing, or other forms. I am talking high-level direct work with Maker spirits. As you will see, I do not recommend that you call yourself a root doctor, professional conjurer, spirit worker, or teacher of witchcraft before engaging on these paths—otherwise fear, shadow forces, grandiosity, paranoia, and a host of other destructive forces will emerge.

Each of these paths flows into and comprises the others in an organic and unending process of self-discovery, recovery, and creation. It is my experience that we have a built-in mechanism in our spirit, soul, and substance life that ensures that at some point we move into and through these paths. It is as if we have an interior direction finder and calibration process that ensures that our life gets what our spirit directs. In conjure, our own spirit has its powerful rhythms and cycles, and they must be adhered to if we are to have happy, healthy, and meaningful lives. The process of being directed from the core of our being is a large part of why we are in this world in the first place. The four ways that our core calls us inward to influence the outer shape of our lives are divine directive, divine restlessness/discontent, ancestral paradox, and elemental paradox. They cannot be ignored without detriment to the worker—or to anyone, for that fact. As a worker for others, I use these callings to diagnose the overall spirit state of my clients.

The Call to the Paths

Sometimes my students speak to me about people who are not on a spiritual path of their understanding. In my opinion, no matter how it appears, everyone is a spirit on a path. If someone is new to their awakening, they will need time and experiences to begin a relationship with this world and the perceptions and influences of their soul within it. We must always use discernment and discretion about how we see other people and their spirit growth. They may not be where we think they are because we are looking from the perspective of where we are. In addition, we are not always clear or honest about where we are. They may be caught up in an area of themselves that is dangerous to others. Quite often we see the world through an inner lens that is formed by outer forms and social/cultural elements rather than from our direct perceptions and insights. Bottom line: too much of our lives is dictated by thought-forms and fundamentalism and not by inspiration, insight, and clarity.

Like a baby getting used to its new body, we may go through phases of our life when we are totally entrenched in the physical world and unaware or uninterested in a greater context. Though I think this is a hazardous phase, it may be necessary for a soul setting into its form or dealing with trauma, fear, or pain. It seems that once our soul is accustomed to being embodied in a human experience, it begins to cultivate its eternal essence (the spirit) through the spirituality, mysticism, and magical practices.

Though many people are called to some form of a spiritual path, a smaller number are on a mystical or magical one, at least consciously. In these two paths, spirit (God, Goddess, all that is) is not directing the lifetime; rather, it is supplying power to the directive of the mystical soul and the summoning forces of the magical will. These attributes are hard-won components of being, embodied by serious inner work. Some aspects of modern religious practice appear to give seekers a context in which to rest their spirit until they are ready for cultivating it through mystical, and possibly magical, practices and experiences. For some, religion is not enough, and they are called to abandon dogma and seek a direct experience of spirit, which is the precursory state to the other two paths. Too often, the call to a deepening of the path is sounded through sorrow that drives us to our soul, or a crisis that breaks our hold on a form of ourselves that is restricting our spirit life. This could be the legendary dark night of the soul or some other stagnation or pattern-shattering experience.

I have noticed that there are four primary ways a human is called to cultivate his or her spirit beyond adherence to fear-based spirituality and to move focus to congruence-based practices anchored in love, wisdom, and power. These callings are based on my experience; they are not being offered as dogma, but as guideposts. They form a direction-finding mechanism for understanding and responding to our own inner voice, spirit, rhythm, and tides.

The calling to the crossroads of change and growth is one of the most sacred dynamics of our life. Sadly, too many of us treat the callings as adversarial, when they are our life force in its four primary modes, teaching and growing us so we do not waste our precious lives in patterns of unsatisfying illusion, entrenchments, and entanglements. They can happen in any order or any combination depending on the needs of your spirit, soul, and body (or other attributes of your physical life). They have their own general patterns or symptoms. I will discuss both the nature of the callings and present a generalized introduction to the symptoms. These descriptions are useful in navigating the life experience from both sides of our heart: the inner/invisible one and the outer/visible one.

Ancestral Paradox

When each of us selected our physical parents as the birthing and building point of our soul into this world, there were several factors that influenced the choice: the needs of our soul for growth and healing in this life; the needs of our species and world that would be addressed by our soul; and the needs of the blood we were born into for healing and growth. Now, this approach to the birth process presupposes a belief in a conscious soul and reincarnation. Both of these beliefs are a strong part of my spirit paradigm. As a part of these factors, each of us inherited certain ancestral issues or paradoxes (problems) that we promised (at the soul level) to heal to the extent of our capacities. Even if we do not believe that we selected our parents and blood lineage, we cannot deny that we were born to our parents and have inherited many traits from them. There are times in our lives when it seems like an inner alarm has sounded and the patterns of our mother and father are appearing inside of us. Rather than curse or fear these patterns, it is best to see this as a call to the center to discover yourself as a part of a stream of life but not to be drowned in it. If we deny or ignore these patterns when they emerge (especially if they are toxic), then we are casting to chaos the potential for healing, growth, and the betterment of our blood. We are not doomed to become our parents' sins. We are charged to heal what we can and pass the best onward to the next generations. Likewise, sometimes our blood is trying to give us a power or potential that has not been unlocked yet. It is sad when we fight our inner rhythms and distrust the life our spirit chooses. I promise that there is perfection in your life experience. It may need to be mined out of you and your experience, but it is there.

Symptoms of the Ancestral Paradox

The primary clue that this calling is occurring is a spiritual, mental, emotional, and/or physical pattern that has repeatedly appeared in our ancestors. Basically, this looks like you are becoming an unhealthy aspect of your ancestral patterns. I often tell my students and clients that these symptoms are a part of your contract with your blood. Each of us was born to redeem or heal certain aspects of our ancestral blood— to receive its blessings and to bless it. These patterns can be physical, financial, emotional, social, mental, or a myriad of other domains of experience. These symptoms feel like the sins of the mothers and fathers visiting the sons and daughters, but it is actually a sacred part of a multigenerational ancestral life.

Elemental Paradox

To get a body, a soul will need parents as a gateway and ges-
tation place. However, it is not our parents alone who supply
our form; it is the larger body of nature herself that makes
up our parents and all our ancestry. Our human parents provide access to the stream of human nature wherein we become
one of the links in a human chain of tens of thousands of years,
thousands of cultures, and immeasurable depth of knowing.
The planetary nature, often called Mother Nature, supplies the
elements of our beloved planet to garb, feed, and fulfill our
human experience. The elements of nature include the biochemical elements, cellular structures, organic components,
and neurological processes (to name a few), and are the very
vessels and life structures for our ancestral blood and personal
soul. These structures must be attended to as well since they
are intimate partners in our human experience. Bottom line,
they are ancient, powerful, and immeasurably intelligent,
and they are the parents to our form. Often, issues with the
body that involve illness, pain, body modifications, or other
changes are a sounding call by the elemental structures of our
body to be in a co-creative experience with them and come into
a deeper life with our form. If we can embrace our challenges
in this area as a voice of direction, reflection, and healing (to
ourselves and others), we truly transmute the experience. Our
natural lives have an inherent perfection even when it is painful.
Our bodies are an honest and constant partner while we are in
them. It seems a shame not to engage it as friend instead of foe.

Symptoms of the Elemental Paradox

Our elemental nature is our planetary composition. It is felt
as the voice of our body. Yes, our body has a powerful vote

in the direction of our life experience, and we must respect its voice. The sensations and feelings our very honest physical partner gives us is the way that the planet's voice (or at least our personal part) talks to us. The more vocal aspects of its voice are experienced in pain and intense pleasure, but these are not the only way we can experience the aliveness of our form. Our physical health states, the maturing phases of our form, and the feelings we have in it are a sacred language about the patterns (healthy and toxic) of our embodiment experience. When we experience this calling, our body is talking to us.

Divine Discontent or Restlessness

This feels like depression or anxiety at times. Divine discontent is a dynamic pulse in our soul that does not allow the soul to stagnate. It is our fluidic energetic life force, the sticky essence that glues our cellular structures into a form for the animation of spirit. It bridges spirit to body and has deep occult tides that connect to the seemingly invisible tides of nature (human and other). It seems to be an inner mechanism that sounds the call to get moving with the process of self-revelation and creation. Divine discontent is our center, or soul, saying, "Come to life." It calls us from our beds at night with questions about who, why, and where we are with our lives. It inspires us to shake loose from the bindings of our soul and make room within us for our own deep voice to speak and direct our lives. Divine discontent is a call to ourselves—a call to our central soul of being.

Symptoms of Divine Discontent or Restlessness

When our soul calls us to listen, it is embodied in the experience of divine discontent or restlessness. Unfortunately, because so little emphasis is placed on the soul's voices in the general culture, the mystical experience of soul longing is often translated as depression or anxiety. This is not to discount the fact that these disorders do exist, but perhaps they would not be so prevalent if more people were mentored on the voice of the soul. The symptoms of this calling can feel like sadness, grief, a call to the interior, a desire for solitude and reflection, a drive to grow and change, intense questioning, or anxiety—a drive to change an elusive something. My mother described this calling as touching her soul.

Divine Directive

When divine directive moves into us, it may feel like the Tower card in the tarot. It may feel like our world is being detonated and destroyed when in fact divine grace has moved in to do the work our personal selves have not been able to do. The highly charged and high-level directive flows down, or out, from the highest (or deepest) places of our spirit and into our souls, and if the shape of our life resists, that shape may very well be shattered completely. Where divine discontent feels like it is coming out of us, divine directive feels alien to us. Many of my students describe it as electricity straight from God. It requires a deep surrender to the will of spirit. It requires immense change and a discovery that we are shaped, directed, protected, and fueled by a vision that is bigger than we have known in the past.

Symptoms of Divine Directive

Divine directive is initially the most foreign feeling of the callings because it originates in the least human and most divine part of our spirit. In fact, many report that it feels like lightning has come down from the heavens, caused change, and suspended democracy. When its power enters into the old shape of our life, it shatters it. A great deal of what is familiar in the pattern of life is taken way. It feels like we are being punished by God, though space is being made within and around us for the vision of our spirit to grow itself. The most obvious symptom is a full-blown crisis that leaves us wondering where life is going. If we make room within ourselves, new vision for the direction of our life will emerge. My mother says that this is a time "when God has planted a new seed in our soul." It is a vision or anointing from both our spirit and the Spirit, and cannot be ignored or avoided.

❖ ❖ ❖

These four callings can be easy or hard for us. The choice is ours alone—even when it appears that this is not the case. Sadly, because the voice of the individual soul is often muted by the requirements of our outer lives, the callings have to get louder and more powerful before (and if) we are to hear and respond to them. This heightened or intensified calling often comes in the form of an initiatory crisis that shatters the confines of old paradigms and life shapes to allow the pulse of the deeper spirit to surface and direct the shape of our lives. I think of this increased intensity like tremors before a volcanic eruption. In this case, the molten lava is the forces of our soul and spirit that spew outward from our core to shape our life into congruency. This eruption can be subtle or earth-shattering, and its effects can be liberating or incapacitating. It all depends on our ability to (as they say back home) "doctor the root." This folk expression refers to our ability to root our lives in our spirit and to grow our life expressions from that foundation. One of the most vital tasks of the root doctor, spirit worker, or conjurer is assessing where individual clients are in this process and how to doctor it into vitality.

The Dampers on the Blue Flame

So much of the mystical path in my work is about tuning back in to the frequency of our own soul and its spirit. I have found that there are four primary inner conflicts or soul wounds that must be addressed to let our soul's voice become clear as the director of our embodied experience. I call these the dampers on the blue flame. The blue flame is a concept that shows up in many witchcraft traditions (including my own) as the magic flame and the power of the deep soul. It is the primary source of the witch's power and though the language is a little different in conjure, the power and truth are the same. When we have prolonged inner pain and conflict that is not rooted in a chemical or organic malady or diagnosis, it is often sourced in one or more of the four dampers. As you read these dampers and apply them as a soul navigation and life interpretation instrument, you may feel tempted to curse the seemingly negative forces in your life. I strongly advise against this, unless you want to feed your forces of dissolution and alienate the potent forces of your soul that are informing you through life's mirror. As my mother told me, "Whatever happens in your life, bless it and receive it, or bless it and send it on its way."

So, how do we get into conflicts with the directive of our own spirit and the rhythm of our soul? In my teachings, it comes when we dampen the flame of our soul's voice. This

happens through one primary soul wound and its four conse-
quential wounds. Let's look closer at the wounds. I discovered
the dampers through many years of self-reflection, healing, discovery, and revelation. As I developed myself spiritually, mys-
tically, and magically, I began to see certain core wounds to
the human soul that were within me and within every person
I loved. It became clear that these wounds, if addressed in the
spirit of guidance and growth, point in the direction of love,
wisdom, and power. If not addressed, they can be destructive to
the quality of life at best, and deadly at worst. There is a saying
that the conjurers that trained me shared with me about looking directly into the face of our own mortality as the source of
spirit power. It goes like this: "You cannot be a conjurer until
death sets on your shoulders and informs you." This very wise
saying reminds us not to waste time fighting our life and losing
our spirit. Rather, develop a relationship with your own spirit,
the shape of your outer life, and the voice of your soul, and then
life will expose its spirit roads and possibilities to you. The four
dampers are: the illusion of isolation, the desire to possess, the
resentment of change, and the desire for absolutes. I will now
go over each one and present some insights into how they are
experienced and what can be achieved by addressing them.

The Illusion of Isolation

The first damper, the illusion of isolation, is experienced in us
as a feeling of abandonment and disconnection from the creator, from the seed of spirit within us and its connections to
the rest of the world, and seen and unseen worlds.

I have observed in my folk tradition that the primary
wound in the human soul is abandonment pain. This means

that the one fear that all humans share is that we have been or will be abandoned by spirit, life, and those we love. This illusion and abandonment fear is a byproduct of our humanness as characterized in our free will. But it is an illusion that we are truly disconnected. After all, spirit is the force that makes up everything. If all things are made of energy, then how can anything or anyone be truly disconnected? It is our perception that gives us the feeling or sensation of unity with life or abandonment from it. To work the root, we must be willing to consciously reconnect to the wholeness of life—whether you call it God, Goddess, the Maker, Spirit, the Great Spirit, or Source Energy really matters not. Those names are forms, not absolutes. There is a big price to our inner world, as well as the world of form on our planet, if we do not address this illusion. It is toxic separateness that leads to madness, ecological exploitation, self-destruction, toxic dependencies, and basic unhappiness with life.

When this pain or its resultant chronic fear is the primary motivator in our lives, desperation is the result. This desperation inspires us to battle life or try to devour it like an over-specialized parasite. We can see this individually and culturally in our species by watching its symptoms on the daily news. It seems that we need more of every resource, which squeezes all the life out of our beautiful planet and our neighbors on it. The only way to heal this wound is by reaching into the core of our being, past the illusions of the surface world and into a place inside us that remembers and knows we are made of pure spirit—that we are a spirit in a human experience. Ultimately, it is the role of spirituality to link the wave of our perceptions back into the ocean of life. We must know through experience that we are not separated from spirit; we are expressed within it. Without this, we will always feel a false exile from the holiness and wholeness of life.

The Desire to Possess

The next damper, the desire to possess, manifests as a feeling of desperation to keep things controllable, predictable, and self-affirming. We are often more comfortable with a familiar pain than an unfamiliar joy—at least it is predictable and familiar to us. With this desperation comes a need for more things, more titles, more relationships, and so on—to possess more as a sort of insulation against change. This builds more of a cage than a true fortress. This damper also shows itself as our attempt to put conditions on hold or in a sort of parking place that often becomes a festering pile of rotting inner debris that is poisonous to our spirit and to those we love or relate to. The more abandonment fear active in a person's consciousness, the more he or she will want to control and possess things, situations, relationships, roles, and people. The desire to possess causes a restriction on the spirit's ability to breathe from the inside out, thus causing eruptions of change and intense levels of discontentment. When this damper becomes toxic, life causes us to prune ourselves of false shapes to allow our soul to bud and our spirit to blossom.

The Resentment of Change

The next damper, the resentment of change, manifests as anger, which may turn inward as depression. This damper arrives within us, when, in desperation, we endeavor to prevent change; when change is imminent, our desperation to control becomes fury. Though somewhat energizing, this damper can cause battles within and without. Often when change comes and a new chapter of our spirit is unfolding, we can get angry at life and the spirit behind it. Mom called it a "temper tantrum with God." This anger keeps us out of sync with our life rhythm and its patterns, attempting to lock us into a state of intoxicating stagnation. As a conjurer, my clients come to me often wanting me to force something to happen for them, even if it is obviously against what is in their best interest. They just want control at all costs. In many cases, this control can be given through magic to this resentful soul, but the cost may be a part of their own soul's offerings to them. It is my job to doctor their root and know when magic is contrary to the dictates of their spirit.

The Desire for Absolutes

The final damper, the desire for absolutes, manifests most often as a steadfast need to be right. This damper wants spirit to have rules and be predictable. Addressing this damper is the beginning of letting our soul breathe. It is being directed by a living spirit instead of a stifled one. Fundamentalism is the most obvious and dangerous symptom of this damper. The overwhelming need (at the expense of compassion or intimacy) to be right is very obvious in far too many relationships, be they intimate, professional, or otherwise spiritual. It is also the source of many "holy wars," inquisitions, and political or religious genocides. There are times when the need to be right even overrides the actual quality, accurateness, and meaningful intention of the information offered in interaction.

Casting Off the Spell of Forgetfulness

All of the material I have presented thus far is to be used as tools for spirit workers to understand themselves as embodied, in-souled, and inspirited beings. Without understanding our own paths, processes, and problems, we are ill-equipped to help our loved ones or clients. Some years ago, I developed a concept I call "the spell of forgetfulness." It refers to a state where we have forgotten our inner rhythms, how to hear the voice of our soul and spirit, and how to translate and integrate our own spirit life. In my opinion and those of my most trusted teachers, it is this loss of self-knowledge and connection with our very life force and its interwoven nature in the web of life that causes the bulk of human suffering. Most human suffering comes from resisting what is.

The roles of the spirit worker or conjurer are to assess, diagnose, and treat the unseen forces of themselves and their effects on the mental, emotional, and physical worlds of themselves and their loved ones or clients. The spirit worker uses lore, techniques, and practices to doctor the root (spirit) of an individual to improve the quality of life and conscious growth of the most eternal component of one's being—the spirit.

The internal directive and character quality of the individual conjurer will influence the ethics and focus of the worker. Therefore, just because a person calls himself or herself a worker does not make it so. Likewise, just because an individual is a worker, it does not mean that person is a loving, caring, good, or ethical being. The good news is that the worker of toxic magic eventually gets visited by the fruits of his or her work. You cannot conjure a spirit or magic power without getting it on or in you. Therefore, no matter how powerful a worker thinks he is, he will be touched by all he touches. If you conjure healing, guarding, and blessing powers, then that is what will eventually shape you and your life. Likewise, if you conjure vengeful, toxic, cursing powers, then that is what will shape you and your life. You make the choice. The crossroads will call, command, and contact all of us.

We must remember that we are made out of the same essence that everything is composed of. We are intertwined with the entire web of life. We must own our place on the web and manage it with honor, humility, grace, and power. The magic of conjure is a sacred art that allows us to be conscious and powerful mini-creators with the larger creation forces. When the spell of forgetfulness begins to lift, the callings become sacred voices and the dampers become reminders of how to heal fear and re-enter the family of creation. If attended well, the remembrance process will help us be worthy to be a part of this earth and her destiny. Welcome to the crossroads. Light your candle and let's make the magic that made the world.

Chapter 3

The Origins of Southern Conjure and Root Doctoring

A spirit worker knows where God's blessings lay and how to pray them out. But, you must make your heart and God's heart the same if you want to call (conjure) the blessings out.

— BETTY JEAN, ORION'S MOTHER

It is improper at best, and impossible at worst, to tap in to the spirit forces of conjure without an anchored knowledge and respect for its history and cultural flavor. Though conjure has core historical attributes and elements, there is no one "southern conjure tradition" because of the diversity of people, practices, and locations involved. No practitioner can claim to have the one true practice. The primary core attribute is its cultural and religious/spiritual foundations. These attributes *must* be honored for conjure to maintain its potency and integrity. This attribute is not debatable. Conjurers can only speak from what they have learned and what they innately know, with additional support (if they want it) from other conjure practices and academic research on the subject. In the conjure information I present in this book, I speak from what I know, from what I learned, and from the practices in my culture of origin. I provide a basis for one stream of conjure. This information is not meant to imply anything orthodox or universal. I have used some academic references, but I am primarily reporting as a person practicing a living tradition taught to him by his mother, neighbors, elders, and other spirit workers encountered in his birth culture. When I say conjure, I mean "my conjure."

Attributes of Conjure

Though magical practitioners tend to use what works and draw from an eclectic menu, conjure is not eclectic. It is synergistic. Its core of beliefs and practices is always growing while never losing its taproot. Its synergistic qualities have allowed it to travel through many threatening cultural encounters, not the least of which were slavery, forced relocation, cultural assimilation/homogeneity, and genocide of indigenous Native American people and their practices. An often overlooked component of conjure is the European pagan (with a Christian overlay) magical practices that were also incorporated into the lore, recipes, and techniques. Though often not as obvious, they do contribute to the taproot of conjure.

This taproot extends deep into hundreds of years of culture, ethnicity, and change in the fertile compost of its history. Then it rises into the blood, culture, and teachings of those who pass it on from generation to generation. In my conjure, this root's primary origin is in African practice. It incorporated Native American and then European spirit work from the south of America toward the north, where it continued to grow into Asian, Jewish, and many other cultures. It shows its face in different places under different names such as hoodoo, witchcraft, root work, and a host of other guises. The conjurer of today is often not born into it or raised around it as I was. In fact, it seems that many cultural and familial ways are dying out quickly. This is the primary reason that I have written this section of my book with a tone of soulfulness, and sometimes even sadness.

The intention of today's seeker of conjure may be sound or insane, inspirited, or self-centered, and it does not depend on the ethnicity, age, gender, sexual orientation, or other outer characteristics of the practitioner. I have seen bad workers (ineffective or immoral) from all ethnic and cultural groups. Ultimately, the ethical and spiritual quality of conjure depends on the content of the spirit, the character of the seeker, and the ability to look beyond the surface of conjure practices and beliefs to the roots, where its power and its directives always remain intact. Once workers go into that part of spirit, they need no approval from a human to tap the root. They have it from living spirit and the conjure spirits themselves. I do think that the novice conjurer would do well to seek guidance from an experienced one if possible, though there are many helpful books and websites with content or information and practice. Failing that, it is important to at least spend some time with someone from a family or cultural conjure practice to learn the subtleties of the practice. There are some aspects that come to a student through the spirit and feel of one who has paved a deep road to the spirits.

Conjure reaches deep into the American spirit (good and bad) and forces a discovery of authenticity of spirit if it is to grant sound spiritual and magical power to the practitioner. Let's be clear: conjure is about power. Power is the ability to effect change. Our ancestors in this work kept conjure alive to rescue their souls from tyranny and keep them safe in the hands of God (the spirit) and the powerful spirits and ancestors of their lands of origin. As the social environment of America went through its phases of slavery, poverty, inequity, and many other dark and harmful forces, conjure also became the power to overcome domination and get access to the good things of life. It granted the magical art of survival. It became a way for workers to doctor their own and others' spirits through working (spells), cleansing, sweet and bitter work (blessing or harming), and healing of spirits—the list of applications goes on. Conjure does come with a caveat—it will force what lies in your heart to show itself, so it is wise to treat it with respect and keep it as clean as possible. The spirits in this work ensure that our own spirit will, as my mother said, "revisit us with our own honey or poison, which we will have to eat." This keeps me in right relationship with spirit and the power it gives.

In some ways, power is a more accessible force to us today than it was for the people in the history of conjure, when people used it to navigate severe inequality and disparity. Racism, sexism, homophobia, classism, and a host of oppressive "isms" still exist, and thus conjure is still a need in many people's lives. Because of the ancient presence of these spirits in African, Native American, and European traditions, and because the route they took to America was one of oppression and struggle, these spirits are of genuine essence distilled by time, change, deep need, and reverence. For this reason, its deep and powerful spirits rise up from the waters of life's memory to aid us, but only if we seek power that comes from genuine spirit within us. We must be seeking to grow our spirits and not to diminish others'. A totally self-indulged worker soon discovers that he or she must help others out of their pits of despair to get the support of conjure spirits; otherwise, the worker is attempting to betray the spirit of these spirits, which will not abide well. For this reason, I always ask spirit to fill me with clarity, inner peace, compassion, and courage so I do well by the blessings of the conjure power.

The spirits of conjure and their respective powers know the spirit of the conjure seeker. Conjurers cannot hide the content of their intentions, nor their hearts, from these deep-rooted forces. The nature of the spirits we attract is shaped by the nature of the spirits inside us. Ms. Granny (who I discuss later) said to me, "God sends conjure that is the shade of your heart." The conjure spirits live at the center of spirit itself and their view and reach is pure and deep. Personally, I feel deeply blessed because the spirits are this way. They keep me honest on all levels, and I praise and honor them for this! The conjure spirits will serve, but they exact a big fee if the conjurer is not seeking their help in ways congruent with their spirit, which is of equity, protection from harm, blessing of the good life, and a life free from harmful domination. In the end, conjure (as a spirit force in itself) suffers no fools or exploiters.

If you are not willing to cry for, be angry for, pray for, and ask help of its spirits, then stay away from this work. These spirits went through hell when they first came to America in boats of flesh. No one can change this root, and why should or would we want to? If you want to find the root that cannot be bound, then the root spirit of conjure is for you. If you want to grow your spirit from a place of truth and spirit power, then conjure is for you. If you want to reach deep and pray high, then welcome to this deep well of spirit and spiritual nurturance. But come through the door blessing and praying for the ancestors that suffered. This builds a bridge of grace to the spirit world and begins to establish the essence and flavor of the spirits that come when you conjure. As Mom said, "Pray for the dead, for they are praying for you."

In addition to its intense history and unique social roles, there are also attributes of the conjure I practice that give some basic insights into how it works and what the worker knows:

- God, or the Maker, is busy with universal life and has many spirits and spiritual beings that can be called on for help;

- Spirit is the root of all things, and it must be cleansed, healed, fed, protected, and "dressed" to grow in this world;

- Power is accessible and the Maker wants us to have it;

- The spirits of the dead continue to work with us;

- There is a crossroads spirit that opens the roads into and out of the spirit world. It is met at crossroads or center-posts such as trees, large stones, high crosses, and obelisks in graveyards or other meeting points;

- We can set the spirit roads into and out of our spirit worlds to effect goodness in our lives;

- Conjure is a spiritual power in all things (also called the root), but it is also the name of a practice;

- Conjure can be conjured or awakened in things such as roots, stones, teeth, claws, and all things of nature, then fed and dressed to do work for the worker;

- Though you do not need to have the spirit sight to be a worker, it helps. The power to be a worker is often in families and bloodlines;

- Fire is the thing in life most like living spirit, so it can be used to give power to workings; and

- A worker works with both hands, meaning she has the ability to help or harm. Remember that healing a disease in a human is a death sentence to bacteria, cancer cells, or viruses. The lines in power are not as clear as one might think.

The Bedrock of Conjure

The conjure practices I grew up around have African, African-American, and Native American foundations. In his scholarly work on the subject, *Conjure in African American Society*, Jeffrey E. Anderson noted:

> Modern American conjure is a mixture of magical beliefs originating in two zones of European settlement, which remained quite distinct during the seventeenth, eighteenth, and nineteenth centuries. The first of the areas to be settled by European colonists was the Atlantic coast, encompassing Maryland, Virginia, North Carolina, South Carolina, and Georgia. The second included French and Spanish settlements, chiefly on the Gulf of Mexico and the lower Mississippi River.

As a conjurer from Virginia who has traveled throughout the United States meeting other workers, I know that these zones have evolved very different forms of conjure. All of them preserve distinctively African elements. There is no way to exclude the African elements of this practice and have it still be considered southern conjure.

If you are racist, this practice is not only wrong for you; it will devour you from the inside out (as well it should!). However, though the foundations are African, other cultures and races are woven into its colorful fabric. There are also many religious and spiritual traditions that lend their mark to conjure as it is practiced today. In the Shenandoah Valley, where I am from, Protestant practices from Christianity and some English, Irish, and Scottish pagan practices were also a part of the cultural soup pot of my conjure. The ways that conjure is discussed and the terms used vary from location to location.

The few times my teachers used the word *magic*, they referred to spirit work (conjure) as soulful magic born from suffering. They were adamant that I understood that its roots came from African slaves forced out of their homelands by slavery while they held tightly to an unbreakable inner spirit and link to God and its attending spirits. This foundation was mixed with other cultures and practices in the New World. These conjure spirits also met the holy and indigenous practices of the First Nations of America, the Native Americans. Both groups were struggling against the tyranny of colonization, and spirit work gave respite and empowerment through this horrific experience. Along the road to survival, conjure met other brethren in the struggle.

The commonalities these intersecting cultures shared were poverty, discrimination, marginalization, and other harsh forces that diminish and limit access to the resources of well-being and the elements of a happy life. And like other forces grown out of harshness, sorrow, and soulfulness such as blues, jazz, and even country music forms, conjure gave power to the spirit. It gave back some of the power stolen through oppression, especially when the forces of the social world seemed to keep the poorest poor and the discriminated oppressed and cast out of equal justice and access to resources. Conjure is a power that comes from a deep spirit beyond the boundaries of flesh and hardship. It rumbles and rises like volcanic lava detonating bondage, freeing inner power and shaping all it touches. It comes from a core that refuses to be downtrodden and cursed by the unjust and greedy. In its flow, the conjurer has the power of the hopes, dreams, blessings, and prayers of those before him in time and spirit. To enter into a sharing with you, the reader, I must share more information on how I came into and continue to live within the spirit and power of conjure and its spirit family.

Honoring My Roots

I honor the spirits of my roots, as they were my entry into conjure in this life. I offer praise to my roots and the roots of their roots. I praise my mother and my many teachers for embedding and enforcing this understanding within me. It is an understanding of my magical, spiritual, cultural, and blood ancestors and teachers, and they must always be honored and blessed. They form the root from which my spirit work grows, and the spirit worker cannot do powerful work without their help.

In the Shenandoah Valley, these types of conjure were not only practiced in the African-American community. In fact, poor folks were poor folks where I lived, and this made it necessary for us to share information for making a better life and dealing with medical issues without the costly medical doctor who was only affordable for folks who lived in town. I learned from my mother, who learned from her Caucasian mother and her African-American godmother. Additionally, I learned practices from neighbors, friends I met at church, and people I met living in the Shenandoah Valley, a place with many layers of cultural influence including Appalachian Celtic, African-American, and European folk magic elements. Many of the workers I knew growing up struggled with their gift as the world was changing around them. Some of them loved the work and praised spirit for giving it to them. Others, like my mother, struggled with their spirit gifts and worried that their children would suffer because of them. Others experienced a mix of feeling burdened by their ability to receive tokens (or speak to spirits) while enjoying the ability to make money with it. They were proud that conjure is an old family or cultural practice and a heritage worth preservation. All of these experiences form much of the deep presence of spirit that fuels the very heart of what I know as conjure or spirit work. The inner-knowing I have about conjuring comes through practices, history, culture, and lifestyle associated with it.

It is from this inner-knowing and historical fact that I call you, the reader, and I, the writer, to pause for a moment of silence to honor the African, Native American, and other human and divine spirits that walked the waves of sorrow to the New World or struggled under the forced relocation from their motherlands. Despite the horrors they endured, today all people whose spirits seek to be one with divine order are able to achieve a good life, to receive their blessings in conjure. You live! Your conjure spirit thrives in those who earnestly seek the deep conjure that grew out of the American South! And our prayers seek to heal your wounds, grow your power, and anchor your wisdom so that needless suffering may end.

May we honor them in our work always and in all days! May we not only pray to them for guidance and help, but also pray into spirit for their strength and healing! That is the way of the spirit worker; there is no other way into direct contact but through a heart that blesses the road it walks and those who walked it before them and through them.

The Role and Spirit of Conjure

As mentioned earlier, conjure shares a synergy with European and Native American practices synchronized with Catholic or Protestant spiritual beliefs and structures. It was and is practiced by white and black folk alike and was not (and is not) seen as a tradition, per se. It was something you did for what you needed. Good and bad people across races and cultures often attempt to make it theirs and theirs only. This false ownership defies the very history and spirit of conjure as I know it. As I have worked with conjure workers from the South and other areas in America who grew up in family or cultural practices, I have been delighted at the many streams of conjure—they are unique, yet similar. Even in the relatively comparable geographic location and cultural groups, practices seem to vary based on family, immigration patterns, and history. There are also differing opinions on the roles and attributes of the worker.

The folks who knew how to do the work were both feared and revered. They were known for their power, a force that could be used to help or harm. In some communities, the conjurer goes to church like everyone else and is considered to be a devout Christian who does this work in service to the Lord. In other communities, the worker is almost seen as the boogeyman (or woman) who lives at the back of the alley, on a dirt road, in an old trailer, or some out-of-the-way place. Folks are warned to be wary of this person and avoid them at all costs. Yet, when times are rough and no doctor, priest, or lawyer can help, it is the conjurer they visit. In yet other communities, the worker is a valued part of the local community, one who has been consulted for cleansings, blessings, charms, and spiritual readings for generations. Some workers glow with the light of spirit, while others are annoyingly grumpy or outrageously showy, creating an atmosphere of intrigue and other-worldliness. Some workers use statues, washtubs, or candles for setting lights, while others do nearly all their work at the graveyard, crossroads, rivers, and old trees. The image and style differs from worker to worker. But there is one thing all workers have in common: if they are real, they link directly into the spirit world and can work the forces of the root (spiritual power) in a way that is direct, often simple, and potent. In most cases, the worker does conjure for a living, and he is well worth his pay. Conjuring is a social role, a magical practice, and a vocation.

The role of the conjurer used to be more confined to the South, though there were magic workers such as pow-wow doctors, witches, granny women, or free-men in other states and sections of America. I didn't know about these workers when I was growing up, though I was aware of granny women, who were midwives and herbalists as well as healers of the spirit. The southern spirit worker has moved northward or westward to many areas of our country and beyond. Spirit work has changed. It has grown. In the not-so-distant past, many of the workers were illiterate and only knew what they could remember. Others learned from their parents, who taught them by reading the Bible. This is why some practices use *thee, thou*, and other forms of what my teachers called the Bible tongue—it was seen as the way God talks, and therefore it had power. As workers had greater access to education, books began to emerge; some of them recorded practices, while others introduced new ones or added to old ones.

The many books on candle magic, prayer, herbs/roots, and formularies for oils, powders, incenses, and so on that filled bookstores and mail-order businesses throughout the early- to mid-1900s also added to the conjure corpus. Today, many people access hoodoo and other forms of conjure and have become workers or dabblers. In some ways this is good; it lets the world in on this potent practice. In other ways it is bad; spirit work becomes another trend, a do-it-yourself system, or just a form of cultural appropriation. I use many of these books, especially the "old-timey" ones. But they were not known where I came from and I did not begin using or accessing them until well after I moved north to Maryland. In this book, I hope to bring the reader back to the foundations of conjure practice before it expanded to include so many other elements.

Chapter 4

The Nature and Power of Conjure

*The power of things is in its root. The root is the spirit,
and the spirit gives the power. The root worker is a spirit
worker. Their (the conjurers') power is of the spirit (God)
and its (his) spirits; and these spirits are in everything.*

—Ms. Granny

As I mentioned in the previous chapter, Ms. Granny was my
mother's midwife. She always wore white. She wore a white dress,
white shoes, and white stockings with a nurse-like white bon-
net. No one really knew the full story of why she preferred
white; some thought she meant to live as close to the purity of
God as possible. The beauty of her dark ebony, aged skin and
her deep and knowing brown eyes made her look like an angel
to me. Perhaps the most powerful aspect of her garb was its
cleanliness—I can't remember seeing so much as a spot of dirt
on her white regalia. When she worked in the kitchen, she was
spotless. When she worked in the garden, she was spotless.

When she butchered the chickens, she was spotless. When asked how this could be, she would humbly laugh, showing her beautiful white teeth through full and sumptuous lips, and say, "Why, child, I am covered in the spirit and spirit keeps me clean; but then your heart already knew that, right, sweet boy?" My eyes fill with tears when I reflect on her and how my short time of less than ten years in her life now shapes my life and those I teach.

Ms. Granny wrote her wisdom on my mother's soul, who in turn wrote it on mine. Now, I pass it to you, and I hope it informs your soul as well. To get to the power of conjure work, you must get to your root. Your spirit (or soul) is your root and your heart is the path inward to the deep places of the root. Conjure work, in its purest form, is passed on as an oral tradition. It is passed from worker to worker through oral lore and techniques. It is passed on by shared experiences that introduce workers to their gift, their own inner spirit, and the world of the spirits. In the end, you cannot read enough books to become a conjurer. You cannot fill your mind with enough data to become competent in the ways of the spirit and the spirits. You have to be willing to encounter the spirit world directly and be remade in the shape God first saw you in.

For those put off by the word *God*, know that conjure is highly influenced by the Christian spiritual tradition. Therefore the word must be used to accurately speak in the language and practices of southern conjuring. When I use this term, I mean the creator however you see him, her, or it. You could use the word *spirit* if you like. However, the Bible was a primary tool of power in the conjure work I grew up with, and even though I am a witch as well as a conjurer, I still use the

Bible in my work. Ultimately, today's spirit worker (in my opinion) must be able to reach beyond religious politics and into the deep abiding spirit in all people, places, and things. To do this, you must be willing to reach into, and live from, your root. You must be baptized in the waters of life and spirit that continuously flow without beginning or end. These alone are the fit waters for the root of spirit.

In my conjure form, you have to go into your spirit to where it meets with all spirits, especially the living spirit of God. This path is inward through your feelings and then outward into your practices. You have to feel your spirit inside, and from that vantage point, you can tap the root in stones, herbs, graves, and even the human and other beings that the spirit worker serves. You have to be a part of the spirit world consciously. Initially, this can be a challenge for students of conjure work. When I teach my students, I am clear that they must do a lot of spiritual cleansing work. I encourage them to do devotional work with Spirit and spirits consistently for a while before they develop the subtle sensitivity to know the difference between their own spirit and other ones. The devotional work ensures that students are covered with power as they grow in spirit and conjure power. Covering is an imperative part of sound, sane, and solid conjuring and spirit work.

In short, covering is an alignment with a stream of spiritual practices (such as baptism, initiation, consecration, etc.) or the guidance and protection of a divine power. You can always tell whether a worker has been exposed to an old style by the language he or she uses, and one of the primary indicators is the use of this term. It is always good for a worker to hear from and be trained by a conjurer. So I offer you advice, much in the language it was offered to me.

Conjure from the Mouth of a Conjurer:
An Informal Chat

I am a conjurer, and an old-style one at that! I work with the Spirit and its spirits. I work with spirits of the graveyard, crossroads, and a host of other types. With the aid of their power and my gifts, I work to help people shake off the dominations that bind their power and block them from the good things life offers. Whether my clients are dealing with a mean-spirited employer, a wife-beating lover, a family curse, or an addiction, I work with the gifts given to me by God (the spirit), my blood (my ancestors), my family of spirits, and the techniques I have learned. I use this power to help and rarely to harm. Before I started working with people in this way, I underwent many challenges to attain sovereignty over my own spirit. By sovereignty I mean the reclamation and ownership of the spirit that God gave me (and you). You and I are made of, and continue to be made by, the source around and within. *This means that the source that is in everything, such as the earth, moon, sun, and stars, is also in you and I.* Though this appears to be an easily understood and embraced truism, few truly encounter and embrace this. Embracing this truth requires serious work on living in the spirit.

When people come to me for help, one of the first things I look into is what or who owns their spirit. I ask them to consider what animates them—what occupies their attention and feelings and thus expends their life force? Everything in our life flows out from the invisible world of the spirit. It is the nature of this flow that influences the roads of goodness and wellbeing to and from us, which leads to another question: What pinches the roads between your own inner spirit and the blessings it bestows and the roads outward into the world of outer form? Knowing this, and taking back the throne within, is what God wants for us while we are in this world. Spirit wants us to grow that into the world while listening to the higher voice of spirit. This sovereignty is ultimately the bottom line of what conjuring, or spirit work, is really about.

My form of conjure is both powerful and spiritual, and it has the potency to help or harm. I prefer to help people with my work. The apparent harming work is also an important subject, for sometimes something or someone who is harmful and dangerous must be stopped.

People come to me with unhealthy spirits on and in them. Often, by the time they come to a spirit worker like me, these spirit forces have caused them great pain and confusion. Sometimes they come because pain has so shaped their spirits that they are being eaten by it. Other times, they are caught at a place in their life that is unhealthy, harming, or limiting them. I doctor their root (spirit) through readings, cleansings, spirit work, mojos (spirit bags), and a host of other forms to get them moving in the direction of a good, fulfilling, and healthy life. Though our world has more technology than ever, the needs of the soul and the spirit seem more foreign and harder to reach. These simple needs drive leaders, politicians, scientists, and spiritual leaders to the door of the root doctor. It seems that though we know more about the world outside us, we know less about the world within us. This leads our people back to their roots, and back to the reclamation of themselves as an expression of spirit with an eternal as well as physical destiny.

In the complex and competitive nature of today's world, I think that spirit work is more needed than ever. Our world is filled with information and activities but has lost contact with the rhythms and language of the spirit. This fast-paced life-style can catapult people out and away from contact with their own spirit. They begin to think that they are defined by their relationships, jobs, lifestyles, and other elements instead of by the spirit life that flows in them. For this reason, I am speaking to the reader from the soul and spirit of conjure so we can get back to our root, plant it in the garden of life, and reap a harvest for ourselves, those we love, and the world around and within us. Conjure has always had a potent simplicity at its foundations—one that is so strong that it can neither be captured nor truly corrupted. Regardless of age, race, creed, or financial or social status, it has a calling and an offering to respond to needs. At its root, it calls us to our soul. The farther out from the soul we live, the more we feel the forces of entanglement, entrenchment, confusion, and disconnection. No matter how complex or technically evolved we become as a species, we will always long for the root; we will crave to feel one with the life within us and to have a purpose in life that includes a celebration of life and the joys it offers. We will change, grow, and encounter the pain that forces us to deeper, truer understanding if we open to God and navigate our lives with the guidance of our soul. This is a primary spiritual directive fulfilled by the spirit doctors of all traditions, and definitely the ones in the South.

To me, one of the most valuable aspects of this knowledge is that it is not theoretical. Without the feeling of soulfulness and living spirit inherent in conjure and root doctoring, the intellectual information has little or no meaningful or lasting effect. What I provide here is practical and direct and from the mouth of a practicing spirit worker who was raised around living tradition. I was introduced from the inside of my conjure culture rather than being introduced to it from the outside. In fact, I really did not know that spirit work (or spiritual work, as my folks called it) was anything out of the normal. I did not see it as occult or witchcraft or anything like that. I rarely heard it called conjure. As I met other conjurers from similar practices and cultures, it became clear to me that spirit work was the same as what is now more commonly known as conjure.

The people I refer to as my teachers were humble but unquestioningly powerful. They were clear that a worker that is living and working in the spirit can make powerful conjure happen—with or without supplies, recipes, or other props. They knew, and I know, that spirit work can bring about miracles if the spirit is right. My teachers made sure that I knew that the Spirit and the spirits could help people if one knew how to work with them and had the heart and soul to see them (and yes, even help them when the spirits needed doctoring). In my conjure world, live and seen people were only a part of the equation. The spirits the worker served and was served by comprised a larger community spanning the array of embodied beings, ancestors, ghosts, and a host of seemingly otherworldly beings. To the worker, all of these beings were in many ways integral to each other and not so much of another world. It was the quality of the relationship between beings and across states of being that resulted in healthy or unhealthy outcomes. The spirit worker was a sort of physician placed here to help human and other people, living, dead, and "other," out of bondage and into a good life. This help could take many forms: it could be cleansing, healing, setting lights attraction, and doing send-back work, or even doing the more aggressive and fierce work of retribution and protection, often called "hot" work.

Far too many would-be conjurers who want to do work professionally only want to do the sweetening work, meaning love, attraction, healing, and so on. All workers—professional or those who work conjure for themselves or their family—will have to do protection or other harsh work. This also means entering into the equivalent of spiritual warfare, if warranted, for the safety of yourself and those you serve or love. Let's be realistic: even though most of us strive to be good, honest, loving, and just people, the human world is not always this way, especially for those who are economically or otherwise disenfranchised. Sometimes conjure work was (and still is) the only safe and equitable recourse. There have been times when my clients or loved ones were truly being harmed by the evil intentions of another living human or a spirit and I had to step in and stop the harm. As a child, and later as an adult, I watched people come to workers despondent and spiritually exhausted; they found healing and wholeness. I also saw the cruel and wicked get properly addressed and incapacitated by the worker's power and spirits. This is not the largest proportion of my spirit work, but we live in a real world where there are parasites, victimizers, bullies, and murderers, to name a few of the harmful spirits.

Addressing this is as much a part of the trade of the worker as baths, charms, setting lights, and other work to bring the elements of happiness to a client's life. If you want to be a worker, you have to look at both the good and evil of the world and make a choice about whom and what you serve. Because conjure in the American South came and grew out of the struggle for equity and justice, I chose to serve the same purpose. I recommend you do the same. Remember this: *the spirits you work also work you.* Make sure that what you conjure is what you want for yourself. There is no way to conjure without getting the power on you. Do you want a bitter or a sweet covering? This is a profoundly shaping question to ponder if you step into the world of active spirit work. This question leads you inward toward your spirit, where enquiry meets the eternal, which is the greatest of all conjure crossroads. The journey to this answer never really ends. Rather, it deepens in its revelations as you grow as a human and a spirit. I do not think I will ever be finished peering into the depths of my spirit and cleansing out the wounded and wounding parts of my own mind.

I was introduced into this work through the heart and soul, not through the head and ego. I saw people in need who were getting help from conjure work. I think this is an important statement to make as more people seek conjure in its many forms, including root work and hoodoo. It is unsafe at best and fully destructive at worst to think that any of us, as one of my teachers stated, "owns da conja" (owns the conjure power). It is owned by its source, even if that source is inside us. *The conjurer conjures from the spirit, for the spirit, and through the spirit. No exceptions, ever!* There is no way to do this work and not have to get right with your spirit. It will force workers to clean out their bad spiritual energies, for we are what is inside us. If, however, workers manage to tap the power and work through a powerful spirit to do conjure that harms for the sake of harm, those workers will indeed find themselves at the mercy of their own spirits. As one of my teachers once said, "If you work a spirit that eats people, don't forget you are a people too." This speaks well to the old saying: "If you lie down with dogs, you will wake up with fleas." (No disrespect meant to our lovely canine friends.) If the would-be workers want to work conjure for a good life, then this work has immense benefits.

If they want to mock God, the spirits, the ancestors, and the gift of the conjure work, then this work holds eventual danger for them. With that in mind, welcome to the crossroads of the conjure work.

Conjure Types and Techniques

Conjure has many forms, but I can only offer the forms that I know and work with at this time. These forms were taught to me at different times in my life. Some of them I learned at home in my original culture. Others I learned later in life. I am still growing in this work and will be until I die and beyond. If I were to write this same book in five years, I would add even more information. Workers are always growing their own spirit and their relationship with the spirit world. The types of conjure and the mechanics of the work vary from practice to practice, culture to culture, and worker to worker, at least in their southern forms. There are a lot more distinct areas of conjure types and techniques that, no doubt, have grown out of the needs of the people it serves. Below are general topic areas and approaches. Under each general area are some of the techniques that my teachers and I feel are core to the competent practice of spirit work.

Working with *the* Spirit

This area of conjure works directly with God, the Maker, the Spirit, or the many names given in the work for the Source spirit. These areas are not engaging with the more personal spirits such as ancestors and crossroads beings. They are working with accessing and directing the blessings of the essence of which all things and persons are made. This area of work challenges workers to reach outside themselves and use prayer, conjuration, and cleansing to get their inner spirits into close contact with the spirit or power that made and is still making everything. Without this contact, workers are in danger of getting trapped in what we call the bitter work of the spirit. This means the harmful aspects of the inner and outer human spirit, both embodied and not (dead). Working in the spirit requires workers to have humility, commitment, and devotion to a constant practice of self-assessment, reflection, and cleansing to ensure that they can hear their spirit and the Spirit. Otherwise, workers may step into a metaphorical hornet's nest with their own weaknesses as target for bitter or ill-tempered and bad-intentioned forces. There are several areas for working the spirit.

Fire Work

The first area is what I call fire work. The basic principle of fire working is that fire is the closest thing to the living spirit in the physical world. Our ancestors first accessed this power by lightning strikes from the sky hitting the physical world and causing fire or the light of heaven to come forth. This was seen as a direct gift from God to humanity, and indeed it changed us as a species forever. The discovery of fire inspired humanity to see itself as a distinct species that could influence its own fate. Fire separated us from the bitter cold. It brought personal light to the dark nights and drove away the animal, human, and spirit predators in the foreboding darkness when our ancestors slept outside with little to no cover. Fire, through cooking, chased away what seemed like demonic forces (parasites) in uncooked meat, which often poisoned us. Fire is warm like the sun, and it seemed colored like it as well. It moves in mystical and transformative ways and has always delivered a change in form to whatever it touches. Thus, to the elders before us, it must have appeared to be God, here and now, straight from the sun, stars, and lightning of the vast heavens. Fire has a powerful grip on humanity at the hearth and bonfire, and it commands respect in its destruction of our homes.

When I was being trained as a witch, I was given one of the most enlightening and insightful quests I have ever experienced. My mother had died and I was preparing to go to Virginia for the funeral. My teacher told me to touch my mother's hand and say what was different about her. I was perplexed but compliant. When loved ones die and we touch their lifeless form, they are cold. Like my beloved mother's body, they feel almost alien from their selfhood. The conclusion my teacher helped me reach was that whatever it is that gives life is warm and fiery. When it is gone, the human form becomes lifeless and inanimate. Bottom line: to our ancestors, this fire was magical, miraculous, and daunting. Even today, the many forms of fire, heat, and light define our daily lives. Thus, the ominous flame still has its grip on our spirit.

In spirit work, fire conjure is primarily done through what is called setting of lights or candle magic. When I grew up in the country, few people had candles. They were expensive, and we had electricity by then. Sometimes outside fires were used. But as I moved closer to the city, the use of candles became more common. Old-time workers taught me how to use the fire in a candle to set light to the work and keep it fired up with power. Fire guided the spirit. When a candle is used, usually it is dressed using one or more of the following methods:

1. "Prayer spit" (spit infused with the prayer of the worker, or other bodily fluids, such as blood or semen)

2. Ashes from Bible verses mixed with olive oil

3. Carvings of prayers into the candle itself

4. Fruit juices or vinegar

The candle was lit to get the power fired up, and then it was fed with offerings of whiskey, rum, tobacco, and other food. These offerings were placed under the candle for the flame to eat as food as it fired up the spirit sent forth by the worker. Fire work will be addressed in the conjure work sections of this book because it is so close to the root of spirit work.

Healing Work

The next form of direct spirit work is healing work. This work seeks to either restore wellbeing or create it in a person (animal, plant, human, spirit); place (location, home); or thing (an endeavor such as a business, church). Healing work is about blessing in the name and power of God from whence the life comes. This work is usually conducted through laying on of the hands after the fire of the living spirit has been kindled or shook up. This means that the worker raises his or her breath to the mouth of spirit through prayer, and may speak in what appears to be gibberish but is known in my culture as the spirit tongue. The worker may suck out the dark forces of what is harming the client and breathe it into the mouth of God by directing it upward and hard breathing it out until the worker feels the spirit take it. The worker then fills up on the spirit and breathes it into the client's body with either his or her own breath or the laying on of hands to confer the healing power. My mother always felt that both the worker and the client needed to be covered. The worker should have cleared the spirit with a cleansing bath and anointed himself or herself with some holy oil, such as olive oil, before touching the client's spirit. In this way, the worker is ready to be covered and filled by the power of spirit. Covering means that a blessing from a higher power or sacred spirit is placed on the client like a covering to prevent re-intrusion of the harm and to set the new prayer in the spirit of the client. Usually we did this by covering our hands with olive oil and praying to God (or the Maker) to fill our hands with his or her power and crown or cover the client with blessings of Holy Spirit. There are other forms of healing in conjuration, but this form is specifically direct Maker work.

Spiritual Cleansing

The next form of direct spirit work is spiritual cleansing. Spiritual cleansing is focused on clearing a person's spirit of harmful and hindering energy and spirits. To me, this is perhaps the single most important aspect of conjure, both for the client and for the worker. Before and after any spirit work, workers should always cleanse themselves, their tools, and the space where the work is being done. This clears all contact from negating, incongruent, and unhealthy spirits and forces. Client and worker cleansing can be done through blessed baths, colognes like Florida Water, teas, herbs, bath salts, fumigating (smoking) the body with cedar wood, tobacco, or other sacred plant materials, or, as I prefer, a combination of these cleansing types. I advise all new workers to research Native American herbal practices. They have given us time-honored and powerful wisdom on herbs for cleansing, including white sage, sweet grass, lavender, cedar, and juniper tips as well as other plant helpers. Most of these herbs were not part of the practices I grew up with. However, other items were used, such as detergents like Reckitt's Bluing or Mrs. Stewart's Bluing and household items like tobacco water, coffee, and vinegar. Bottom line, as my mother would say: "We are always stepping in something." Therefore all people, workers or not, should be in the practice of doing cleansing practices and covering themselves.

Praying True

The next form of direct spirit work is praying true. First, I must state that I am clear that everyone can and should pray. In fact, I feel that prayer is vital to the wellbeing of our spirit. Prayer is how we lift our spirit out of the entanglements and entrenchments of the activities and traumas of human life to the cleansing, healing, and blessing power of spirit. It is how we plug our small selves into the big self that created us. In fact, we are still in the process of creating ourselves, and will be until we merge back into the fullness of spirit. The elders in my community implied that praying true was gifted only to a few—those born with it or who received it through some form of spiritual grace, such as a near-death experience, a direct encounter with spirit, or an anointing into some type of ministry. My mother, sister, and I were all born with this gift per my grandmother. However, in my experience, the ability to pray true, which is simply the ability to ask for spirit for something and get it, is accessible to anyone if they develop their spirit. Many times we get hurt, scared, and confused and need someone else who seems to live in the spirit to pray for us. Even workers will get other workers they trust to pray for them when they feel too weak to reach the spirit and bring it forth. Often that person is a preacher, minister, or root worker. This is a part of the trade of conjure. Through praying true, the conjurer conjures forth blessings from God to the client or to a situation or place. I feel that all workers should be able to do this form of work because the need can arise when a worker has none of the usual materials for a spell or conjuration.

Power of Blessing

There is another form of direct spirit work that uses prayer but should have more attention given to it, and that is the power of blessing. Blessing work is usually centered on protection and covering. Clients often come to me wanting their baby, marriage, or some new endeavor blessed against harmful spirits (or as they called it back home, bad washing). Bad washing is when a person doing magic washes another person's luck away or ties it up somehow by washing the victim in bad blood (conjure power). Sometimes, in the course of life, we may garner jealousy or ill will from others, and it gets on us. Blessings are a way to prevent this from causing harm. I also find myself asked to bless objects such as keys, rings, necklaces, or even homes and cars to seal the spirit in them against harmful intrusion. Remember, spirit is in everything in root work. In this work, nothing and no one is truly dead. Everything is alive. Usually the worker will enter a light type of trance (or rapture, as my mom called it), and through prayer or the spirit tongue they access the stream of the "Maka's Blessing" (Maker) and place it into something or on someone. The worker will usually rock back and forth until the blessing power comes upon him or her and then will sort of blast it into wherever it needs to go. Sometimes a worker prays hard until the power comes and then spits in her hands and uses this as living word to place the blessing. The saliva carrying the power of the prayer is then used like anointing oil and is placed on the person or object to be blessed.

Prayer Cloths

A particular form of working with the spirit that was performed in my church as well as by private workers was the making of prayer cloths. This practice was done more in the churches than in homes, but my mother and other workers I know made them too. Prayer cloths are strips of white cloth torn or cut in strips from a sheet. The strips are then anointed by the preacher (minister), elder, or worker and prayed over by the congregation (if in a church) or the worker or groups of workers to heal the person that wears them. They are tied around the affected area, if on a limb like an arm or neck, or folded and placed against the skin of the wearer to heal afflictions. The wearer keeps them on until the worker assesses that the cloth has finished its work or a new one is needed. My mother referred to this as "very old-timey healing work." I find it to be very powerful and useful. Sometimes I will put hyssop oil or tea onto the cloth to protect the client against any escalation or new harm from intruding. Remember, "Hyssop droplets on my arm; what hyssop touches, none may harm."

Working with Spirits

In old-style conjuring, there simply is no way to do this work without the unseen company of the spirit world. The worker knows that everything we see originates in what we cannot see. Matter comes from invisible energy. Our human life is sustained from breath, and breath comes from the air that we cannot see.

The world of the unseen is so much greater in scope and power than the seen one. For the conjurer, these unseen but felt forces are called spirits. In the worker's world, absolutely everything that appears in the mental, emotional, social, and physical world originates in the spirit world. To be spiritual in this work, the worker must relate to God (the Spirit), the influences and powers that carry the spirit(s), and the worker's own source spirit.

The spirit world is filled with these spirit carriers. They are known by many names, such as ancestors (human and other), angels, nature spirits, faeries, deities (in non-southern conjure practices), and so on. There are whole traditions and practices associated with specific spirits and how they work—how to call and release them; how to build, sustain, and feed a relationship with them; the nature of their power; and how to pass them to other workers that we train. I work with several powerful spirits from various spirit types. It is common practice in conjure for the worker to work with a host of spirits. These spirits come to the worker in many different ways. For the purposes of this book, I am delineating the spirits into four major areas: the personal spirits, traditional spirits, nature spirits, and the spirits I call the qualities or principle forces. These categories are not a part of any oral tradition. The only classifications I have ever heard old workers use were terms like *evil, good, protective, godly, demonic, hot, sweet, attracting*, and a host of other qualities but they did not classify them in this way. I am hopeful that this addition will be useful for the old workers as well as the new ones.

Personal Spirits

Personal spirits may include spirits passed to the worker by a mentor, through family tradition, or acquired in very personal ways by the conjurer. I have many of these types, including Marie Laveau and Chief Blackhawk.

Many of us have been influenced by the conjuring and Voodoo spirits of New Orleans, Louisiana. Marie Laveau was a Voodoo priestess from the early- to mid-1800s who was renowned for her spiritual and magical work. Most New Orleans and many other workers work with her powerful spirit for love, justice, healing, and magical knowledge.

Blackhawk was a Sauk Native American Chief who died in 1838. He was a figure in the spiritualist churches in New Orleans and many workers, including myself, work with him for justice, legal, protection, and healing.

The ancestral spirits of dead human people are the most prevalent form of personal spirits employed in conjure working. These spirits may include powerful deceased workers, family members, and others. This area of work may also include broad areas such as law, health, and luck that involve acquired spirits that were not known while embodied and were reached by the worker through "adopting" a graveyard. This practice required working with the aggregate spirit of the entire graveyard (instead of individual spirits), which we call "Daddy Death." Second only to God or Jesus, the ancestral spirits are the most popular spirits among the workers I know. They are the closest to the living and often the most invested in our daily incarnate lives, especially if they knew us when they were "alive" (embodied). I put alive in quotation marks because all magic workers quickly learn that aliveness is a much broader concept for us than it is for the general population. Just because people have died in flesh does not mean they are dead in spirit; just because something is no longer in form does not mean it has lost its power in the spirit world. This was tangible in the Civil War battlefield I grew up around, where you could feel both the spirits of the people killed and the power of the events themselves written into the inner fabric of the place. The spirits of the ancestors are very personal for the worker. They are not usually broad in scope. They are specific. They do not reside far in the heavens. They live just on the other side of our breath in a current of life very close to our own. For this reason, I call them personal.

Graveyard work is both a traditional and personal form of conjure work. It is personal in that the graveyard spirit may be someone we knew in life, or it may be someone interred in a graveyard where we work. It is important that the novice worker understand that the body of someone continues to radiate its own power and life even if the soul has left. This power is accessible to the worker and is a treasure house of information when tapped correctly. Graveyard dirt still holds the power and knowledge of the person buried in the grave; this power can be tapped and used to help the living (embodied) without ever disturbing the soul that has moved on. The graveyard is an absolutely bottomless source of spiritual power. After all, there are more people dead than alive, or as one of my teachers says, "There are more people living below the horizon than above it." The spirit current in the soil is greater than that which is growing on or out of it.

Every day we are physically eating the ancestors to receive the nutrition of life itself. Nearly everything we eat is either a plant, something living in the soil, or an animal that ate plants. The plants draw nutrients out of the soil, which is made of rotted organic matter—including human bodies. Life eats life, and thus there is an unseen but felt bridge between what we perceive as alive and dead. In my work, I recommend people see life in three primary states: incarnate, or in a body; discarnate, or no longer in a body and in the form that most people think of as dead; and non-carnate, like angels, faeries, or other beings that have never been in a body. The spirit worker knows that it is unseen forces that determine the final destiny of things. All of us know that the unseen forces of thought, feeling, perception, and experience influence most outcomes, often regardless of the physical attribute. Therefore, the worker is in partnership with beings that live on what I call the inner tide. The inner tide is the subtle levels that can only be felt, heard, or sensed, but rarely seen or directly touched. I say "rarely" because the spirits touch us all the time, but the dullness of our senses often stops us from experiencing it. The worker courts the spirit world of companions, coworkers, and even family members and in addition to gaining power, gains knowledge of and sensitivity to her own inner spirit.

Traditional Spirits

Traditional spirits are spirit beings with very broad powers. They are known by most workers. I designate these beings into two subgroups: the holy spirits and the conjure spirits. The holy spirits are those that are commonly discussed in the churches. In traditional conjure, they are the spirits that give the power of spirit work as well as the protection against those who abuse spirit power. All workings praise and implore the holy spirits to grant their power and blessing in the work. These forces cover the worker with blessing, power, protection, and guidance. They raise the spirit and the will of the worker to a level where other holy forces can bless and protect them. These forces may be angels, prophets, saints, or spirits washed in the blood—in other words, attuned or consecrated by the overarching power of Spirit. The people I knew who did conjure when I was a child could not read very well. They worked the Lord's Prayer or Psalm 23 to bring them to the throne of God, and then they simply gave themselves over to the power and let the spirit work them.

There are a few holy spirits in the lore I learned growing up in the Shenandoah Valley—God, heaven, Jesus, and sometimes Moses. The primary spirit is called God by most workers and is usually revered as the trinity of Father, Son, and Holy Spirit. God may also be called Old Maker, the Lord, the Great Spirit, Spirit, or a host of other names. Works always start with praise and adoration of God as the source and sum of all spirit. The worker will praise and devote the work to God while asking for his power and direction in all work and bringing the worker to the throne.

The concept of the throne is very important. The throne is basically a state of trance or consciousness where the spirit of the worker and the Holy Spirit come together. Once the spirit of the worker feels the living breath or word of God move in, the worker is ready to conjure forth that power into the work.

Often the Bible is also used in this work. Some of the Psalms are applied as ways to speak with the tongue of God because, according to tradition, anything spoken in the name of God through Jesus and written in the Bible must come true. This tradition comes from the belief that the Bible is the word of God. Likewise, *thee* and *thou* and other such words are considered Bible language; thus, this way of speaking has power. As one of my teachers said, "This is how the Bible speaks, so this is the way God speaks; this is the way to bring power to your spirit work." Interestingly, when I was a child, I was instructed to be mindful of what I read aloud from the Bible because creation would obey it. This was a Christian and spirit worker's way of saying, "Be careful what you wish for, because you may get it."

There are other holy spirits that are also aspects of God. The most well-known are Jesus and the Virgin Mary. I did not grow up in a Catholic family or community, so the Virgin Mary did not figure much in our conjure work. Jesus and Moses were most often the holy names called to bring power. Jesus and the power of his blood were mostly called for blessings, power, and protection, as it was felt that anything asked in his name would come to be. I was taught that calling down the blood of Jesus was to be saved for the most dire works, for it was powerful and irrevocable. Second to Jesus, Moses was called on for power against all foes and to invoke the law upon those who were unjust. Here is an example of one of the prayers I learned:

> *Oh Moses, who delivered the Jews out of the hands of the*
> *Pharaoh;*
> *Oh Moses who knows the laws of God the Father;*
> *To Mount Sinai, I send my spirit.*
> *Hear my voice and by the power of God; throw down*
> *your staff against the false staffs and let those wicked*
> *serpents be devoured.*
> *Come down from the mountain and cast the tablets*
> *upon the wicked.*
> *Give me your power to fulfill the will of God and the*
> *coming of the Blood of the Lamb.*

As you can see (and probably feel), these words are very powerful. This way of working is not mainstream Christian practice. It draws from something older, deeper, and more inspired.

Some workers also call Peter, the keeper of the keys of heaven, to open the way to the good spirit power. This leads us to the concept of the door to heaven. One of the practices of Saint Peter is to reach your hands to heaven. This is called "knocking at the door and reaching to the Mana of heaven." In this practice, the worker says something like this:

Peter, Peter holy man;
Open the gates with your holy hand;
God said you could and well you should
Open the Gates to the Holy Land.

This should be spoken while looking skyward and knocking at the gate of heaven. You can also use an old-fashioned skeleton key and hold it toward the sky above you as to unlock the blessings of heaven. In this practice, workers conjure until they feel like heaven has come closer to them; then they envision a door descending and them placing the key into its keyhole. When this happens, the workers sense the door opening and a shift in spiritual presence.

Once workers feel a response in the shift in spirit, they raise their hands and feel the power descend into them. If they do not feel it, it means that the gates are not open and they have not approached the throne yet. Until this happens, the Mana, or power, is not present to do the work. I was taught to say the Lord's Prayer and wait until the Mana would fall. This felt like heat in the hands. Another way to bring the power is to sing this prayer:

Let the Manna fall Lord:
Let the Manna fall!
Hear your children call, Lord!
Let the Manna fall.

There are a couple of other holy or Biblical spirits that our workers are called to. One of these is more commonly known among workers as Archangel Michael. The other is the Three Holy Magi, who brought gifts to the birth manger of Jesus. The Archangel Michael was described to me as the light of God in heaven and the great protector of mankind. He should be prayed to in the name of the Trinity for protection and truth. His mighty sword can cut through illusion, harmful restrictions, and the ill wishes of all enemies. As far as I am concerned, he should be a presence in the lives and households of all conjure workers. With Michael either blazing the trail before you or standing protective at your back, all work is guarded and the spirit of the worker is both protected and, as my mother would have said, "kept true."

I only heard of workers calling to the Three Holy Magi a few times. Since they honored Jesus with gold, frankincense, and myrrh, their magic was included in God's blessings. Therefore, these three enigmatic figures can be called upon to teach the worker secrets of magic and the wisdom to wield it.

Other spirits figure prominently across most forms of conjure that come from or are affected by the practices of the American South. These spirits are either pivotal to contacting and working with other powers or spirits, or they appear most frequently in conjure as I know it. Neither of these lists (traditional and personal spirits) is exhaustive, but they do give you a feel for the range of spirits that workers may engage. Examples include very broad and powerful spirits that show up in many forms of conjure:

• The Dark Rider, who lives at the crossroads;

• Daddy Death, who guards and guides the spirits of the dead and rules the graveyard;

- The not-so-popular evil spirit called Daddy Down-There;

- The "Johns," which are the spirits in high, low, and Virginia John roots.

The Devil

In my opinion, there is one traditional conjure spirit that crosses over into both witchcraft and conjure practices. It is the guardian or spirit at the crossroads. This particular spirit is the subject of the inquisitional trials of witches, where it is erroneously referred to as the "Christian devil at the cross-roads that the witches seek for magic." The concept of the devil at the crossroads was popularized in the language of conjure by the blues music of Robert Johnson in his hits "Cross Road Blues" and "Hellhound on My Trail." Back home, the people who told me about this incredible spirit called him the Dark Rider at the Crossroads. The Rider devil guards and guides the place where humanity and the rest of the spirit world meet. Not only is he *a* traditional spirit; I consider him (second only to God) *the* traditional spirit. In chapter 9, I will provide more details on his natures, the four points of the crossroads, types of crossroads, and the ways to call and pay him for help.

The next and very famous of the traditional spirits is what my teachers called Daddy Death. Known as Papa Guédé in the Deep South of America, he is the Grim Reaper in other tradi-tions. He is the spirit of death, and in many ways, the cross-roads spirit for the life-death intersection. In all graveyard work, he is the spirit that opens or closes the way to reaching those persons who have moved from the world of form into the world of formlessness. He has access to all of the wisdom of the ancestors and the graveyard. There is no way to enter into his city (the graveyard) and slide into the dimension of the spirit people who live there without his blessings and guidance. I feel that Daddy Death helps us see the death current as a stream of powerful, deep, and holy power—a mystery that all of us will encounter at some time. When I lead my students to the graveyard and they expose the bones of their fear of the dead, I feel they are closer to revealing their power than ever before. In chapter 8, I will go into depth on ways to work the death road. When the Daddy's ways are truly understood, the gates of life truly open to the conjure worker.

One of less-than-savory spirits in the conjure world is known as Daddy Down-There. Daddy Down-There is the spirit that many recognize as the Christian concept of the devil. I do not recommend that my students work with him; however, I do think it is important to understand him. I was introduced to him by an old-style worker when I was about fifteen years of age. Daddy Down-There lives at the center of the crossroads but under the ground. He is composed of all the anger and hatred of everyone ever planted in the earth at burial. He really is evil in that there is nothing connected to him that is related to goodness, blessing, or wholeness. He is the unrequited spirit who is never happy. I have been trained on how to bring him out of the dust, but I will not write about this. He is dangerous, and once he is petitioned, he never fully goes away. Once he gets his fingers into the crevices of your soul, he never really lets go. Once the worker has decided that Daddy Down-There is the spirit to give him or her power, there is no turning back. That is a crossroads better left closed. To any readers who think they are big and bad enough to take him on—you are delusional.

Root Spirits

The final groupings of traditional spirits I will mention are the people who live in the root. In most cases, when I speak of the root, I mean the spirit. However, there are spirits that live on the roots of certain plants that present themselves in many of the conjure practices of the South. These roots are the roots of plants. They represent a type of fetish magic wherein the root is a house for a particular spirit. These roots are believed to be the dwelling place for spirits that traveled over from Africa during the forced importation of slaves. Some writers have developed whole legends about how those slaves came to America. I can only tell you what I heard, word of mouth, from workers in Virginia and throughout the American South. The primary botanical roots that were taught to me are as follows:

- High John

- Chewing/Spitting John

- Virginia John

The most famous of these "Johnny Roots" is High John, which was called Good Johnny Root when I first heard of this root and its spirit. It is what is commonly called John the Conqueror, or as they say in the conjure worker circles, John-Da-Conker Root. The root usually sold under this name is a form of jalap (*Ipomoea jalap*), which is related to morning glory root. It is my belief that the jalap may not have been the original home for this spirit. Rather, the spirit of High John may have dwelled in other roots before he made his way to this root. The spirit of Good Johnny liberates the one who calls him from domination and any form of shackling and slavery. In chapter 10, I will give specific information on finding the root, waking John up, feeding him, and dressing him for spirit work.

The next Johnny Root that I work with is Spitting John, also known as Low John or Galangal Root. This is the only John root that can be eaten without toxic effects. It is called Spitting John because in the old days, the worker would chew it and then spit the juices on the floor of a courtroom to achieve the winning edge (not advised today!). This root is also worked to achieve financial success. Often, it is chewed and then its juice is spit into one's hands before shaking hands for a sales or contractual deal. It is also used to lean the spirit of good fortune toward the wearer.

Another root, known as Virginia John or Trillium Root, is also used to lean the spirits of good fortune toward the worker. In the valley where I was raised, it was called Snake Root and was also used to avoid the poisonous ways of those who wish to cause harm or restrict one from having the winning edge in gambling, betting, or negotiations. There were pink-flowered Snake Roots that were used to beat the competition of another person seeking your lover's attention. The yellow-flowered ones were used for general work, and the red-flowered ones for pure power. I have found that all of these Virginia John Roots give a winning edge to the worker.

There is one last grouping of spirits in conjure work, which I call principle forces (though they were never really called anything when I learned about them). They can be found at the crossroads or the graveyard and can even be influenced by the roots. They deserve attention as forces in their own right, however.

Principle Forces

The principle forces are those related to qualities of life. I will discuss them briefly in this chapter because they will be interwoven into other parts of the book. These spirits embody the good things in life. The principle forces are encountered on the four roads that intersect at the crossroads: life, death, luck, and love. These are very broad classifications, but they include such things as health, prosperity, relationships, justice, endings, cleansings, and a host of other qualities and virtues. The principle forces are conjured through crossroads work, graveyard work, spirit bags and lucky hands, container spells, and a host of other ways of work, all of which will be discussed in the forthcoming chapters. Now that you have tasted the nature and power of conjure, let's move into a deeper and more intimate relationship with the spirit world of this conjure man.

Chapter 5

Growing Your Spirit

If you don't have your spirit, then you have no spirit. So, you got to get right with your spirit to be right with any spirit.

—Ms. Granny

The most important spirit those who seek to be spirit workers can ever conjure to this world is their own. Without it, we can never feel an enduring satisfaction with life. This spirit is our root, and in my opinion, it is the most important focus of root doctors, when they are assisting clients. To understand this aspect of spirit working, let me share what I discovered while working with my apprentices.

Over the years, I have had the honor to train and mentor hundreds of spirit workers from all over the country and abroad. In this wonderful process, I have been privy to incredible people while they seek and reveal often astounding experiences and discoveries. This continues to be an invaluable opportunity for me to be taught through witnessing the many expressions of the living spirit though its people. I have also witnessed a puzzling pattern in many of the students and even teachers I have known. Most of them have voiced a desire to grow spiritually, learn about magic, and/or develop the use of their subtle senses (also known as intuitive or psychic abilities). These desires are very powerful and important aspects of cultivation of spirit. However, they are, in my opinion, neither the core nor primary drive of our truer quest. They are benefits of the quest but not the drive or primary intention of it. The core drive is actually easier to find, closer to reach, and more constant in its presence in our lives. Perhaps that closeness is what makes it so elusive, initially. The core drive behind these desires is a personal relationship with their own spirit. Nevertheless, my apprentices report that their understanding of their spirit is often minimal and all too esoteric to be of practical use. This is sad, "for what shall it profit a man, if he shall gain the whole world, and lose his own soul?" (Mark 8:36).

I define the desire to grow spiritually as growing through the application of spirituality as a practice or approach to reaching this aim. Spirituality is a broad concept referring to any practices and paradigms specifically related to spiritual understanding. In my work, I generally define spirituality as approaches (mental, emotional, and behavioral) to understanding and relating to the essence of which all is made, generally known as Spirit. My students were clear that they were not talking about growing in their adherence to a religion, though they may have had one. No, they were referring to something more personal, intimate, and less connected to a scripture or dogma—something that would define itself as they actually encounter and experience Spirit in their own lives and in their own interactions with it. I am not inferring that there is anything wrong with these religious expressions of spirituality, but my students tend to already have a religion, have changed religions, or have no interest in one. Rather, they are looking to have a direct, individualized experience with the creator or Spirit, regardless of the directives of an established religious practice.

I feel that this desire is an important step in having a life-altering and deeply gratifying experience of the holy, the wholeness of life, and its beautiful source, Spirit. It is spirituality that imparts wisdom to the seeker of Spirit because it is anchored in experience of what can be described as divinity. When spirituality is present in a religious experience or practice, then, as my mother would say, "it is anointed." When it is not present, then the religious practice lacks depth, blessing, and enduring effect. I realize I may be stepping on toes with that statement, but I stand by it. It has always been my hope that we never let our religions get in the way of our spirituality. God was here before and will be here after the existence of any of the forms of tradition we refer to as religion. Religions must be more than tradition. They must be alive with spirit to have enduring richness and meanings deeper than fear, shame, or conversion to an accepted group norm. Further, by living spiritually, these students have demonstrated that they want to understand the ways of the creator and to live in a right and meaningful relationship with it. This is a noble and beautiful intention. However, it lacks a key component that is very important to the achievement of the intention behind our very creation. This component is related to the creator inside or at the core of us. I feel that conjure practices provide deep insights into understanding and relating to this core.

These students (and dear companions on the journey) had almost never said that they knew that they are a spirit and that they wanted to grow this quality of their existence into the fullness of its life and power. They understood that there are attributes and practices that they could develop in their mindset and lifestyle that would help them attain a relationship with the Spirit or God. Then they could use the power to get what they wanted from God through conjuring work or magical techniques. Sometimes they were clear that they believed that magic was related to the mind and its workings, and that it was also related to spirit. However, they were not clear that everything about them, including their minds, originated in their own spirit, which is a stream or spark of the Spirit, which is the source and sum of everything and everyone. In fact, the very component of their being that was integral to everything about them was the one attribute that seemed most distant in the conversations. This approach is like wanting to study about the lungs but not breathing while doing it. (We know how well that would work!) Ultimately, the understanding of spirituality that is most valuable to us is in how it informs us as seekers on the nature of the God spirit that created us, and therefore, the part of God that is us. Why should we read information on Spirit, spirituality, and disciplines and practices that can affect it? Because we need the information to get the brain's attention in order to focus on the most pervasive organ of our existence . . . our spirit. It must be from the position of our own powerful spirit that we approach the other spirits we seek.

The Most Valuable of All Spirits

The important understanding that was missing from the discussions is that the brain, and in fact all of the human body from which mind arises, is the product of an invisible force that is felt in our aliveness and in deep feelings. Our inner spirit is the most powerful spiritual influence in our lives. Too often, the apprentices inferred that their spirit was only about thoughts and intellectual processes and that more or specific information alone would somehow induce their sensitivity to and understanding of their spirit. Sadly, this is a major misconception regarding the development of the inner spirit. Yes, information and practices can inspire deep feelings and inner sensations of our spirit. This hopefully will inspire the "feeler" to a connection to a deeper, richer, more unified, and whole state of being. But the information alone will not bring Spirit or your personal part of it (*your* spirit) into focus. This type of focus is composed of attention, which is direction of our efforts; discipline, which involves consistence and maintenance of direction; growth, which is experienced as expansion or extending the reach of our spirit; and fruition, which is experienced as the revelations received during the refinement and discovery of our inner spirit's creative capacities. Of course, I am stating this while writing a book to provide information, which may seem like a contradiction. Yet it is my intention to inspire soulful feeling and practices that further stir this feeling and its power to create. This feeling is a very special one—it is an attribute of the "soul," which is another way was labeling the personal spirit of us. So what is the most important spirit in our lives? The answer is our own inner spirit! It is the jewel of our quest.

Everyone reading and writing this book *is a spirit* in a human form. We do not have to find another spirit to be the core of our lives when *we are the spirit in the core of our lives.* We are spirits that have come into the world for reasons to be explored and revealed in our individual and collective life paths. We are spirits in and of ourselves, seeking revelation in the physical expression of our life experience. The closest statement to this that my students usually make is that they know they have spirit *in them* and that they want to know how to work with it. What is missing is that personhood that is seeking is also that which is sought. It (your spirit) is seeking to be revealed and grown in its own power, which is why it attracts the brain's attention to magic as the art of conscious creation. The pulse that drives us as seekers and students is a desire to get our attention in line with our spirit, so that the life we live is congruent with the life that is at our very core. For successful and meaningful conjure work, we must understand that our own brain thinks it creates itself when it is actually the instrument for something deeper and more profound: the Spirit that created and owns it. The inner part of that is our spirit.

To grow this spirit, we must assist our brains in understanding that it is a valuable tool when its attention and servitude is to the living spirit within us and within itself. However, when our spirit is silenced and only used as fuel for the brain, danger is imminent, especially if we are reaching to other spirits without being in touch with our own. In my understanding of southern conjure, the reclamation, growth, and sovereignty of our own spirit is the purpose for all of the spiritual and religious practices, beliefs, and disciplines. But this may require us to befriend and attune our outer awareness to this deep abiding presence. Our brain might fight us with over-complication and distracting details until it relaxes and allows its deeper capacities to surface. There are many incredibly valuable ways to do this, including prayer, meditation, breath work, simple rituals, and presence work. Initially, though, most people find that there is a tendency to look to every other spirit form or type to the neglect of the one that is inside us and calling us to hear and obey it. It is almost as if, through spiritual and magical practices, we are inviting the invisible eternal brain inside the cellular one to come forward and be the driver of our consciousness. As we do this, we heal, clarify, nourish, and empower this process of mining out the diamond at the center of our core.

The Mystical Thing

In the plethora of spiritual media available to the seeker, there is a lot of discussion about spirit guides, totem animal spirits, deities, beings that are intimately involved in the exploration of the realms of the spirit. People report going on quests for power animals, seeking or evoking angels, and other work that involves looking for the power, wisdom, and love of other spirit beings. They speak of forces seemingly outside of themselves that are involved in their lives. They ask me how to cast spells, call to the spirits, conjure angels, get in touch with nature spirits, and so on. They may mention that they want to remember their dreams or discover their past lives. Strangely, however, they almost never say that they want to understand their own spirit, right here and now. Yet, when we grow that part of ourselves, reaching to these other spirit beings becomes safer, clearer, more powerful, and delicious with sharing. These other beings can help us grow the vitality and power of our spirit while we help them do the same. Even though it may appear that the intrigue of connecting with these amazing beings is the mystical thing we seek, ultimately it is not. We are seeking something or someone to lead our attention back to relationship with our spirit. These otherworld cousins can help our brain come out of the state of forgetfulness about the spirit level of life where the most animating forces of life reside.

The greatest leap in consciousness for us is when we realize that the spirit we seek is the one that we are. This incredible force can guide, guard, and bless us in the most miraculous ways. Our connection with it is the ultimate salve to the wounds on the soul incurred when we feel abandoned or exiled from the wholeness of life and the spiritual force that creates galaxies. Our spirit is being created by the great pool or web of Spirit we call God. This creation process is constant, and our inner spirit requires the breath of God to be healthy and the interaction with other spirits (in and out of bodies) to reach into itself and be inspired to create. After all, God extended the part of itself that is you and me into creation because God wanted to know something about itself it never knew. It could never know this part of itself without its creations. God explores its creativity through the creative expressions of its creations, and that definitely includes us humans.

We should strive to be in deeper contact with this force within ourselves, which is truly driving the direction of our lives. Too often seekers want rituals, lore, and techniques that put them in touch with Spirit or nature. They rarely want to know the nature of their *own* nature beyond what makes their mind tick (which they discover through the wonderful sciences and interventions related to psychology). It's almost as if seekers of Spirit see the aim of their quest everywhere but inside their own aliveness—they skirt around the edges of the very thing that is summoning their awareness into awakening. Does this sound like you? All of us find ourselves living from the edges and forms rather than the core and the force. It's just a part of the in-built mechanisms of human nature. Eventually we find ourselves unfulfilled no matter what we fill our heads and homes with, and we either enter a crisis to crack us open and get our attention or somehow get a perception of the mystical thing that is so close, yet so elusive.

This mystical thing that calls to all of us is the very essence from which we are sourced. It made us, and is still making us, and is growing itself through our life experiences all the time—even right now. It is a spark from the original fire of life we see as God or Source. It is the pulsing, living spirit that is in us—that *is* us. It is the part of God that looks out through our eyes and discovers and grows itself through our choices and actions as cells in its body. It is the free will of God exploring itself (though it is hardly free for the humanity that expresses it). It is a blessing, but one that requires constant contemplation and discernment on our part if it is to contribute to both the wholeness and the unique discoveries of the living spirit. It requires our attention to develop its expression into this world. As my mother said to me when I was a child, "God put a piece of himself into each of us, and it is up to us to mine it out and place it into the setting of our lives. We are to grow it in our lives because it is a perfect seed from God's own garden." This essence requires our attention, just as our physical body requires water, food, sleep, exercise, and the other components to bodily health. Our spirit core has its own needs and they must be met, or that core has the power to drastically affect our outer lives until we do what God brought us here to do. The bottom line is that when we live in the Spirit, our spirit will fill us with life.

Basically, the spirit that dwells in us is the last frontier sought by most seekers, when it should be the first. If we are losing our spirit, then our joy is going with it. If we are gaining it, then the wonderful dimensions of our life can grow, because ultimately we do not have a spirit—we are Spirit centered into substance! I always recommend to my conjure students that there are two major areas of Spirit that must be priority for them regardless of path, tradition, religion, or practices. All paths that we seek related to cultivation of a relationship to the all-pervasive powers of Spirit must address these two major areas:

- A relationship to God, the source Spirit, the field of consciousness, the wholeness of which all partake and its many attributes and expressions

- A relationship with the part of God that is in us, our inner spirit, for it is our keyhole into the door of the infinite

Anything we do in life that promotes or encourages these attributes serves the unity of life and the interdependency among its seeming parts. Any thought, action, emotion, or relationship that takes us from addressing or honoring these two areas is cause for concern and can be potentially toxic or harmful. One of the rather unique and definitive qualities of southern root doctoring and conjure as I know them is that they focus on both of these in practices such as cleansing, growing, and applying the power of the spirit. This work focuses on a major fact: *your own spirit is your primary spirit guide and helper!*

These are modern and even New Age terms, but I think you understand my point. Without the discernment of your spirit and a brain trained to obey it, work in the spirit world is perilous. Yet it is too often the least fed and focused on as an actual entity in and of itself. The next few chapters of this book are about techniques, practices, and recipes for the care and development of your own spirit before you reach to any of the other spirits addressed in the previous chapter. Let's look at the concept of Spirit and some ways to embrace it.

What Is Spirit?

There are probably as many definitions or concepts of what Spirit is as there are brains attempting to reduce it to a concept, but many people refer to it as God. I will not attempt to define it because this state of being is preconditioned and was formed prior to the development of the central nervous system. I can only share what I know in my heart and inner spirit through personal experience. I can, perhaps, humbly point you in a direction that might lead you to your own experiences. We can only really approach the Spirit from textural concepts, qualities, and even happenings. I implore you to use what I propose only to stimulate you to allow yourself to feel Spirit's presence throughout your life and embedded inside you as your inner spirit. Invite your brain to reach down to your heart and invite it (the heart) to speak to the brain about its life and its wisdom. You will be amazed at what begins to happen as the soul flowers in the radiance of your quest. Our heart has a deep memory of the oneness of Spirit, which can further lead us to where it is seated within us as well as its all-pervasive presence.

You do not have to find your Spirit, because you can never lose it. You only have to give it attention and commitment in your life. For its presence to be strong in your awareness, you must exercise a link with it consistently. The link happens when a bridge is built between the heart and the head.

You cannot grab Spirit because it has and is you. The very fact that you are reading this book means that it has already summoned your attention inward by stimulating interest as an animating force in your brain. I happily offer congratulations to your brain for crossing this bridge and coming to the crossroads. The power that flows through all of these components of yourself is your inner spirit, the personal aspect of the Spirit. It is both the perceiver and the perceived. It is easier to allow the awareness of it to rise within our own consciousness and feelings rather than to ever think we can define and stabilize it into any structure when it is in, through, and beyond all structures. As soon as we invite the Spirit (through prayer) and our inner spirit into our attention, they (it) come with joy and tears, filled with homecoming and sacred longing.

All structures, be they intellectual, sensual, physical, or other forms, are merely Spirit expressing itself and flowing. It is always in motion, yet still and peaceful at its core. Its force presents itself through breath and starlight, space (movement), and essence (illumination and aliveness). In order for us to even reach for an understanding of it, we must already have a memory of it. That is, we cannot crave for that which we have not tasted. Therefore, reaching for the nature of the Spirit only requires us to make room in our life for it to reveal its potent inner tides and wisdoms.

As one of my teachers once explained it, "Spirit is the great web of being, and it includes the threads and the spaces in between as well as the force that weaves and creates the web itself." But where does religion fit in? Well, religion is a doctrine and "relinking discipline" for relating to and understanding the Spirit. It is guidance offered from others such as Jesus, Mohammed, Buddha, and the Hindu prophets who have encountered Spirit and attempted to help humans develop a personal relationship to it. Most often, this guidance is detailed in holy books or other forms of written and oral tradition handed down from the pioneers of that path. That is how I interpret the primary directive of religions, regardless of whether they are always in line with this vision or not. As long as any religion is adamant that it is the one that is right and definitive, it is likely that it is missing the mark that Spirit is alive, growing, not finalized, and all-embracing. However, encoded in all religions are useful insights for keeping our own spirit in relationship with the larger field of Spirit, which the spirit worker calls "God." These spiritual philosophies inform us to reach for the power of Spirit inherent in its wholeness, including such attributes as love, compassion, honesty, unity, service, and a host of other qualities that strengthen God in all its parts—human and other.

What Is Our Spirit?

Once again, the personal spirit within us is as elusive as the larger pool of Spirit we call God. However, I have developed some metaphorical ways for describing our inner spirit (hereafter referred to as "our spirit") and its relationship to God.

- Each of our spirits are sparks from the bonfire of the creator seeking to return to the original flame.

- Our spirits are like waves on the living ocean of being that rise and fall in and out of the sea of God, guided by powerful seen and unseen forces.

- Each of us is a hand mirror in the hand of God looking at itself.

- Each spirit (incarnate like us, discarnate like our dead beloveds, or non-carnate like angels) is a stream out from and back into the pulsing heart of God loving itself.

Perhaps one or more of these may give you contemplative material to inspire a deep feeling or soulful understanding of what your spirit is. Our spirit is always in the presence of God, even if our outer attention has strayed into forms, roles, relationships, and activities that lead our awareness away from oneness with it. When we give our attention and commitment to a consistent relationship with our spirit, it becomes more and more obvious to us. We begin to literally develop a feel for it. The feeling is its language; it can rise in our senses, dreams, inspirations, visions, and sudden knowing; it can create synchronicity that appears in our lives relative to our prayers, meditations, dreams, and conjure work. When this happens, there is a clear dialogue between our spirit and the spirit in all things (God).

Assessing Our Attunement with Spirit

Through years of experience growing my spirit and dialoguing with other workers, I have developed a short checklist of symptoms and experiences that suggest that we are either being summoned to attend to our spirit or we are out of alignment with it. This list is not exhaustive. It does, however, provide you with some clues about what it feels like when your spirit wants your attention. I recommend that you read the checklist of questions and see if they apply to you. If several of them do, it may be time to attend to the needs and directive of your spirit and God. I call these questions ways that Spirit rings the doorbell to our minds. They are mechanisms for getting us to turn our attention in the direction of the spiritual domain of our lives and respond to our current mystery.

The Checklist for Attunement to Our Spirit[*]

Do you feel mentally, emotionally, or energetically exhausted, overwhelmed, and confused without a diagnosable reason?

This may mean that all of the forms, roles, and requirements of your daily life are causing spiritual power to hemorrhage from you. This is like having a hole in your energetic gasoline tank. Many people I have worked with describe this state as feeling off-center, stretched, in a haze, or overstimulated. It often simply means that you need time to unplug your attention from daily requirements and re-plug into the greater energy source of Spirit. Our outer lives have beauty, meaning, and power, but they can never match the energetic nutritional value of Spirit. There are recommended spiritual interventions for this state as follows:

Each day (if possible), retain five to ten minutes in the morning and at night for prayer and meditation. Wellbeing of the spirit begins by turning your attention to the Spirit. The most efficient way to maintain this is through prayer (speaking to Spirit) and meditation (listening to it).

Pray in the morning for the energy and direction you need.

Pray at night for the clearing of your mind and spirit to make room for spiritual energy, comfort, and guidance.

When you are feeling stretched and overwhelmed, remember that your breath is the same breath as the word of God.

[*] This list is not appropriate for clinical assessment and diagnosis. In fact, if you answer yes to many of these questions, it may be useful to seek a clinician for assessment and treatment of any potential physiological or mental health disorders. *No information or techniques in this book are a replacement for clinical intervention.*

Simply think about your breath, and it will bring you into divine presence. Let your breath draw you away from outer business and into its gentle rhythm.

While in prayer, ask God and your spirit to show you where you are losing spirit and to call it back to you. You may have your attention and the feelings it inspires connected to persons, places, or things that are draining your life force.

Do you feel like you have no sense of purpose in your life even if you have achieved most or many of your life goals?

This may mean that your inner spirit's voice has never been given as much credence as the voices and expectations of persons around you. This often makes one feel like no success is gratifying. It may simply be that you have not discovered a way to discuss with your spirit and God what you want of your life in a way that allows clarity, direction, and integration of who you are to flow from you into your outside life. It may only require the following:

Keep a log of the guidance you get when you pray. You can think of these logs as field notes for the soul.

Your spirit needs food like your physical body does. Leave room to attend church, synagogue, or other religious services or integrate prayer, meditation, yoga, or some other form of energetic attuning and feeding time for your spirit to unfold.

Allow space in your life for simply communing with your spirit and with God. Sometimes it may require more intensive time than your daily practices. You may need quiet time to go on retreat or a type of vision quest so that Spirit can speak to you without the demands of daily and outer life.

It is easy to lose the value in what we do in life under the pressure of what we feel we must achieve. You may need to see a spiritual advisor or reader to help you make sense of the discussion happening between your center (your spirit/soul), the source/God, and substance/the physical dimensions of your life. In short, your life may be turning another page, and you may need to make adjustments that reflect who and how your spirit is today.

Do you feel a deep loneliness even when you are in loving relationships with family, lovers, or friends?

This is a classic spiritual dilemma. This means that God (the greater oneness and how it flows within you) wants your attention. It also means that your spirit wants the attention of your outer life. Ultimately, there is no relationship in the human or physical world that can replace this one. Once you understand that no human person can give you the relationship and companionship that you are seeking, you can enjoy the gifts that they do bring into your life. Relationships can summon forth a feeling for your own spirit and its relationship with God. Many of the old mystics reported that nothing brought them any satisfaction but being with God. They literally craved companionship with God. In many ways, absence from the spirit is absence from true life. All physical persons, places, and things are impermanent, but Spirit is eternal. We all crave the feeling of always knowing that we are never alone, and that can only come at the level of spirit, yet that is the one presence that is never away from us.

Maintain a daily conversational prayer life with God. When you do, you are engaging in the relationship that is present the moment you reach your heart to it. Prayer is not meant to get Spirit to you; it is to get your awareness in the direction of Spirit.

Look for the living Spirit in everyone and everything. It is the pulsing life and beauty in all persons and things. Maintaining awareness of it is a salve to this loneliness.

Invite softness into your time alone or with another, allowing Spirit and genuine presence to arrive. You cannot grab Spirit. You have to invite it lovingly and allow its subtle nuances to arrive in intimacy with yourself, with others, with God, and with silence.

Are you always in fear that you will be abandoned by anyone you love?

Feelings of abandonment and the illusion of isolation are the core wounds to humanity. They are a sort of side effect to the quality of spirit we call humanness. The primary causes of this fear are the human ability to think outside of perfect balance, intuition, and instinct; and the human drive to find oneness and eternal presence in outer forms and connections. The second cause is very much an illusion, because no other person or spirit can substitute for the oneness within (or our spirit) and the unity with life (God) that is truly constant and unchanging. These causes are a part of the human mystery. It is because of them that we are; however, it is also what makes us human, inventive, and always in search of answers. We see and create distinctions in the web of life so we can explore them. Unfortunately, we can also get caught in these consciousness threads and become entangled in illusion.

Make the love of spirit your primary relationship. This will prevent you from clinging desperately to others in the physical realm for validation of eternal presence and self-worth.

Pray to God to help you see yourself as it saw you when it made you.

Understand that the link to spirit is the only one that never ends. Forgive form for its passing nature and allow it to reveal its beauty and artistry to you to enjoy but not to own. This invites inner spirit and its outer expressions to reveal itself.

Ask your spirit to fill you with a love and peace that surpasses all understanding. Remember that joy is a state of being that is not contingent on outside inspiration. Declare to yourself that your inner joy is not up for grabs.

Consider that you are also feeling wounds of the past—from the soul level or from your family or culture. Some of your pain may not even belong to you. For this reason, cleansing and ancestral work are also an important part of the cultivation of your spirit.

Do you feel dissatisfied with life even if the outer forms suggest that you have all the good things?

We all want the pleasures of life: health, love, prosperity, happiness. Everything outside of our spirit can inspire an inner response feeling and even delight our senses. However, these things alone do not reveal the deep beauty, inner peace, powerful wisdom, and knowing revelations of the spirit. They can inspire our spirit to be creative, to expand, and to affect the world around us, but they do not complete the spirit or replace it. However, if you look at the spiritual nature in every aspect of your life, then the outer world can be very inspiring, entertaining, and creative indeed. When you feel this form of longing and emptiness, then you are receiving wise council. It is not for you to abandon anything in your current life unless you already want to. It is for you to give space for your spirit to guide you on what it wants you to do next.

Dissatisfaction with what appears to be an otherwise very good life indicates that a soul mystery is presenting itself. Get readings to look at what your soul is saying.

Do what I do: pre-dream/post-dream work. By this I mean make the last thing you give substantive thought to before going to sleep a question to your spirit about what direction you need to take with your life. Make the first thing you do when you wake up be writing down whatever comes into your dreams, regardless of whether it makes sense. After a while, guidance will come. Making room for the guidance in the inner life of the dream world is a powerful way to befriend your spirit.

The easiest intervention is to pray to God for guidance and then become present when it arrives. God is *big*. God is in everything and every place you go. Watch for the subtle guidance like the wording on a road sign, a billboard, a song on the radio, a commercial or show on TV, or the many other tongues that God (Spirit) might use in its web of interrelations.

Too often, we expect our roles, relationships, responsibilities, and other worldly items to complete us. They can only inspire us. Look for the blessings they bring and what they give you; then invite your spirit to show you what it wants you to experience to inspire it to create the next painting on the outer canvas of your life.

Do you have a sense of dread and doom even though life may be fine all around you?

There is a part of us that clearly knows that our mortal life is just that—mortal and impermanent. This is a good awareness to have. Without it, we have no inspiration to receive the blessings of each moment and expend the offerings of this lifetime with discernment, presence, and creativity. Without the understanding that our form is going to die, we do not get to the task of living. If we are not doing what God wants of our spirit and our spirit wants of our life, then we feel like we are out of sync and the achievements we have are meaningless.

Invite service and connection to the wellbeing of others into your life. Maybe you are receiving money, health, loving relationships, friendships, or other blessings, but you are never giving without an expectation of reciprocity.

Consider that your spirit is hungry for a connection that has nothing to do with usual human roles and responsibilities. Maybe it wants you to experience the wisdom that homeless people can share when you help them; perhaps it wants you out of your head and into your heart with no expectation of reward or benefit. Pray for spiritual love and compassion; go clean up trash from the local park; or volunteer at the food bank or homeless shelter.

Life changes, and regardless of whether we understand it, God knows what she/he/it is doing. Pray for clarity and serenity to rise into your awareness and teach you how to embrace the tides of change in the world. Be an agent for its perfection.

Do a spiritual cleansing bath and dress yourself with extra virgin olive oil that has some hyssop, myrrh, and frankincense in it. The spirit of this oil is one of consecration. It will help your energy to rise to the level of your spirit and bring your brain with it.

Do you feel a desperate drive to seek more achievements, experiences, relationships, and material things to have and to own, while never feeling enduring satisfaction from having these?

There are no achievements in the world of form that can give you deep and unmoving self-worth, inner love, or a feeling that you have arrived in the world. Self-worth ultimately comes from knowing that you are a direct creation of the same God that created and is still creating the universe. It comes from knowing that you were an intentional creation and a part of creation's destiny and, therefore, had worth from your very inception. Ultimately, your worth is not defined by your worldly achievements—unless they bring into your heart a feeling of leaving the world more whole, more unified. When that happens, your inner spirit feels like it is in unified voice with God. It does not come from achieving the illusionary perfection of meeting other people's expectations. However, it can flow from our spirit into our awareness through acts and intentions of love, compassion, service, and healing. These actions and intentions invite wholeness to the world. This quality is very much a part of the personality and the inner spirit. There are some activities that we can engage in that inspire our spirit— not just our brains and our physical senses. Our spirit loves beauty, meaning the depth of the soul and its celebration of life and its many forms, which in turn is a celebration of the artful beauty of soulfulness in the world.

Look for beauty and blessing in what you already have present in your life. Often we find ourselves looking for more and more stimulation to feel alive. We feel that the more other people endorse our worth, the more we will feel achieved, beautiful, appreciated, and impactful. Most often, we have already left a mark of beauty upon the world but are not seeing it because it is right in front of us.

Cultivate gratitude in your daily reactions to life. When you awaken in the morning, be grateful and say that out loud to God. Quite often, the projector point for the next level of our spirit's growth is in receiving and celebrating what we already have while holding the quality of joyous expectation in our feelings for what is to come. This is a type of faith, but one based on what we have, not on what we have not.

Often we feel depleted or uninspired by our lives because we are looking forward or backward but are never really present in what God and our own spirit have provided for us. The moment we direct our brain to look thankfully all around at what we have, we begin to live in a heartful, soulful way. This feeds our spirit and invites it to show us more.

Do you feel a resentment of change any time it comes into the orbit of your life?

One of my teachers once told me that most human suffering comes from resisting what is. I have found this to be very true. Life and Spirit are continually moving in an outpouring discovery of beauty and potential. Spirit lives as one specific form or pattern for only short times before it changes. The nature of the creator is to be creative, and it expresses this through ceaseless creation. However, because there is a tendency for humans to feel abandoned or exiled from the perfection of Spirit, there is also a tendency for us to feel like that which is unpredictable is somehow harmful. This causes us to resist the rhythmic tides of Spirit—which, of course, is futile. The tides of life flow in and out of the heart of Spirit. Unless human interference comes into play, we can trust the perfection of our lives to unfold. This is especially true if the spirit worker or person living in harmony with Spirit is in a consistent co-creative relationship with it.

Daily or otherwise consistent relationship with your spirit and God invites a directive from both levels of being to enter our attention. When this happens, our outer awareness is able to respond to this guidance as familiar and powerful. Resentment of change in most cases suggests that a person has been ignoring the guidance of Spirit or the flow of the in-out rhythm of Spirit. Consistent cleansing, covering, and prayer work mitigates this avoidable tension.

When the forces of a new pattern begin to unfold from our spirit or present themselves as a directive from God, it is always useful to open ourselves up to higher guidance. One way of doing this is to pray with our eyes heavenward and speaking our request for guidance while pulling our shoulders back and lifting our heart to heaven. This invites grace to open the heart and allow it to be fed by God and lifted to grace. This technique signals our soul to take charge over the fears of our brain.

Resentment of change is a very useful sign, because it directs our awareness inward to the life flow and away from life-forms. I always advise my students to embrace this aspect of divine discontent, which gives room within and without for the directives of Spirit.

Do you have a constant commitment to being absolutely right in your perceptions while knowing in your core that you are frightened that you are not absolutely right?

The desire for absolutes is an indication of a fear of change. It suggests that a person is afraid to be wrong or, more accurately, afraid to be judged by someone or something as unworthy and shameful if he or she is inaccurate. There are few absolutes in life that can or have been proven to be absolute across time, space, and conditions. History has demonstrated that our culture was absolutely convinced that the world was flat, and now we are absolute that it is not. Perhaps one day we will be absolute that the world is actually a shape that changes with its needs. Life and spirit move, change, and breathe. If we are to live in Spirit, then we must relate to its hidden ways and means, not react to it with futile resistance. In spirit work, the worker often uses the tools of the trade to assist the client in making way for the good things in life by aligning daily life with the inner and godly life.

The need to be right is not the same as knowing your information and the most appropriate and correct action to take. The need to be right has a desperation connected to it that relates to a desire to be in control simply for the sake of control. It feels very punitive or violating to the person you may be attempting to control. They may be pondering to themselves as to whether the not-so-creative debate or argument has any real worth to healing or effective action. When you feel this need rising in your shadow, disengage and turn your awareness inward to your breath. Then, invite yourself to become still and let your spirit reveal to you an action that promotes the most good. Also, demonstrate to the person you are arguing with that you see his or her value (the value of his or her spirit) and seek the answer together.

The need to be absolutely right is a late-stage symptom of fear-driven awareness. In most cases, it is a cry for attention. When I see this arise in myself, I say a prayer to the Mother Spirit: "Holy Spirit, help me to see me as you saw me when you made me."

A need to be right is a call back to alignment with God. In fact, fundamentalism is a major symptom of a broken and fearful alignment with spirit. Compassion and clarity are major attributes to pray from God into your spirit. By the time this force arises into our awareness, our spirit wants us to shut our mouths, get humble, and open to its peaceful and clear power.

The essence (or Spirit) of God is in everyone and everything.

Do you feel deeply ashamed and judgmental of your human needs or human flaws, even though those persons you love or respect value, love, and accept you as you are?

When, no matter what we say or do, we feel dissatisfied with our lives, our soul is calling us to hear its voice. This feeling arising in us is a call inward to discover the next chapter of the unfolding of our spirit. It does not imply that you have failed at anything. It is a type of wanderlust of the soul that drives us to translate all we have done into the insights of our soul. Often it is not the forgiveness of others that our spirit wants of us. It is the forgiveness of our self by our self. It often takes more courage to move on than it does to self-punish or self-destruct. Being overly judgmental always indicates a wound of the soul, and compassion is the salve for its healing.

The farther we stray from contact with the Spirit and our spirit, the more we see self-rightness as a desperate need of our ego. In fact, the worth of our whole identity can become poised on this slippery slope of existence. Active prayer and journaling of the inner guidance we receive helps us break out of this stagnant and destructive pattern. All of the aforementioned recommendations fit for this soul mystery.

Next Steps

Answering yes to two or more of these checklist questions suggests that your spirit is calling your attention inward. If after doing the cleansing in chapter 6 coupled with some of the practices offered in this book you do not feel some consistent relief, see a clinician. The following questions are merely indicators of divine restlessness or divine discontent. You can use them for pondering your quest:

1. Where is your spirit? Attention tells your spirit where to go—do you manage your attention? I advise that you do a regular inventory of what and who occupies your attention. Your findings will inform you as to where your spirit is depositing its power and, thus, your life force.

2. What do you feed your spirit? How do you sustain, animate, or motivate yourself? Though many of our recreational pastimes are fun or delightful to our body and brain, they may not be nutritional to our spirit. The first step to feeding your spirit is caring for your body with nutritional food, consistent hydration with healthy water, and sleep. Then your brain and body have what they need to engage the subtle forces of the soul. The spiritual cleansing, prayer, meditation, ceremony, and other soul-engagement disciplines are then the priority for the growth and power of the spirit, and they must be as important to you as eating or sleeping—or perhaps even more so.

3. Self-displacement: where are you? Often our body, mind, and spirit feel weakened, overwhelmed, or agitated

because our attention is flowing and anchoring into the past, the future, or other leaking places in our life. This may mean that spirit is leaking away through an identity of self that is placed everywhere but within. I call this "self-displacement"—our thoughts are stretching our life force away from our inner-being. Most people have the bulk of their awareness in constant reflection or resentment of the past or anxiety about the future. In my view, the past is for reference, not residence. As long as you are living in the past, you are always dying. As long as you are living in the future, the gift of the life-giving *now* is being drained. The past is good for context and the oncoming *now* (the "future") is useful for goal-setting. Call yourself to having most of your awareness poised on the powerful present and you will begin to own your spirit.

4. Thought-form and fear addiction: are you trapped in a movie running through your head? Recently I heard someone say that we are being force-fed a diet of fear, and this has been my observation as well. The amount of fast-moving change coupled with the instability of the economy and ecology invokes a primal fear for survival. These cultural and environmental threats added to the chronic fear that comes from feeling disconnected from spirit can cause us to become addicted to fear. Yet there are far more sustaining ways to animate and motivate ourselves to grow and change than fear and its sister, destruction. Likewise, we may find ourselves running from self-image to self-image built upon

the expectations of others to find the source of our own spirit. This leads to addictions to images of our self that are bound to change and then induce further fear. A very important aspect of spirit doctoring is the ability for the worker to cleanse off these thought-forms and unhealthy spirits and clean the soul of terror of abandonment so that the inner spirit can grow, flourish, and attract the blessings life has to offer.

It has been my experience that a great deal of soul loss and dis-inspiriting occurs when we overidentify with the multitude of self-images that flow through our head. Each image forms expectations that we place in and upon ourselves, requiring a deposit of our spirit to give it animation. These overly specialized and highly pressured images and expectations drain us of joy and peace and are usually driven by a fear of abandonment. These forces are very destructive and require inner and outer healing and cleansing.

What Does Our Spirit Want of Us?

I have developed a stage model for looking at what our spirit wants of our outer awareness. This model is only a tool for assessing where we are with relationship to our spirit and God. When I do root-doctoring work with ongoing clients, no matter what they report as their outer desires or needs, I always reflect on where they are in these stages. Because of this, the long-term healing and empowerment that the client receives is more enduring and satisfying. The stages are as follows.

Stage 1: Healing

Identifying the painful and limiting parts of our lives in the spirit of excited expectation and healing rather than desperation and foreboding. This includes internal areas of illusion, self-destructive forces and behaviors, and entanglements of destructive patterns.

Stage 2: Revealing

Reach to the Spirit and your inner spirit through integrative practices, prayer, and meditation as well as root-doctoring work to reveal the knowing powers and potential of spirit. As long as we exist, we are never done discovering and revealing the many facets of our soul, the most valuable gem in our lives.

Stage 3: Knowing

Consistent work with our spirit allows its language, inner tides, and directives to surface into our consciousness. This flow brings forth knowledge of who we are at the deepest, most profound levels of our spirit.

Stage 4: Growing

With each step in the growth of our spirit, a new step will present itself. Through this dynamic, we are never complete in knowing and growing our spirit because it is in the life of God itself. This constant process is what true living is all about. It is life that comes from a greater source into and through our inner-being that continues on and on like a river of light. The first stage starts when we ask and allow our spirit to come forward into focus in our lives. We continue to fortify our spirit with contact with its source and reflection outward onto the canvas of our daily lives.

❖ ❖ ❖

The more spirit we have, the more power we have!

Chapter 6

Baby, You've Stepped in Somethin'!

If ya step in somethin' and ya don't clean it off, you'll track that nasty stuff wherever ya go.

Ya gotta clean it off your feet, and your path, if you are going to make good things happen in your life.
—ORION'S MOTHER, BETTY JEAN

This quote came from my mother, who was a powerful example of spiritual strength and power in the spirit. I remember being very young and seeing a man coming to her and discussing his problems. He was having a run of bad luck that was pervasive, debilitating, and disheartening for him and his family. He reported that no matter what he did, it seemed like he could never move ahead in life—that the bad luck seemed to follow him. He said that he prayed hard for release but nothing ever changed. He was depressed and potentially suicidal. He simply could not continue his life with the constant barrage of hardships and setbacks. He was fatigued, broken, and despondent, and no one seemed to be able to help him. His preacher told him that it must be God's will and that he must simply trust God. Luckily for him, he saw how weak his preacher was and had some inner sense that this pattern was not what God wanted for him. He just needed competent help, and that's what my mother was providing.

Mom said to him, "Let's see who sets above you." This means what spiritual power is actually covering or flowing to a person. She looked through her spiritual eyes to assess his covering and said, "Baby, ain't nobody setting above you." Further, she said, "You ain't got no faith, and faith is the bridge over which miracles trod." How powerful is that statement? She pointed out that he had "stepped in something" and it smelled real bad. She told him to "clean his feet" and get new shoes. This was a folk way of saying that his ability to travel in the direction of a good life was affected by the spirits and spiritual power that was currently on him. Bottom line: nothing was going to change until this bad power was gotten off him and a new destiny was fixed to him. He had to get his old path "off his feet" and open a new road in life. The faith part of her assessment was about his ability to maintain a spiritually powerful life. Without this, there was no way for God to be invited into his spirit. If his inner spirit wanted a new and better path in life, it meant that God would have to send a divine directive that would break him open so he could rebuild. That's where the spirit doctoring comes in. He could prepare his life and his spirit for the happiness he desired, but it would take work. He would need faith. He either had to be broken open through a severe crisis or near-death experience, or he needed his spirit doctored. He got the latter from Mom, and his life changed for the better.

Spiritual Cleansing and Clearing: The Most Important Step to Root Doctoring

The most important, yet too often overlooked, aspect of conjure work is spiritual cleansing and clearing. There is a plethora of recipes and instructions for cleansing our homes and spiritual spaces (i.e., temples, altars, etc.), but little is focused on the most important energetic and creative leveraging point we have—our own spirits. In fact, in far too many cases, once root-doctoring clients make their way to my door, they are in a chronically unclean state of spirit that has left them nearly despondent, exploited, deeply depressed, anxious, sleep deprived, and plagued with a host of other symptoms. They want to jump in and change how the physical world appears to them. For the competent worker, this is like putting the metaphorical cart before the horse. It is important to know that our physical lives will follow the flow of our spirit. That flow may be deeply entrenched in patterns, entangled in unhealthy and harmful relational webs, and wrapped in an energetic cocoon that prevents a person from moving into a happier state of living. This is where spiritual cleansing and clearing comes into play.

Spiritual cleansing is a process by which unwanted influences are removed from the energetic field (spirit), and its vitality is fueled, fed, and strengthened. Concurrent with this process is the cleansing of our homes, cars, offices, and other places that may nest and shape spiritual energies that are not in our best interest.

This process is imperative for general wellbeing and must be an integral part of any spirit doctoring if a new pattern is to be achieved. I recommend all people, spirit workers or not, have a personal process for doing this on a regular basis. I will provide a step-by-step method for cleansing that uses some of the methods I have learned. I will also give further insights in the crossing and uncrossing section later in this chapter. The bottom line is that if we want to manage the blessing roads of our lives and grow our spirits, we *must* initiate and maintain a practice of energetic and spiritual hygiene.

Managing Your Spirit-Path

Your own inner spirit is the most important one you have. An essential aspect of directing the growth and power of your spirit is negotiating your spirit-path and the shapes your spirit takes in this world. This means managing how your spirit grows and discerning the spirits that it relates to. The spirit-path is a pathway of power that has to be managed like any other pathway, or else it will get closed, cluttered, pitted, or impeded. Our discernment involves how we maintain our paths and our presence in this world, and how we guide the direction of our own life force in how it shapes itself. This shape then expresses itself onto the canvas of the world of form through the four roads of the crossroads. This discernment has to be managed by good self-assessment and ongoing energetic and spiritual practices. By the time most people come to a spirit doctor, they have well-trodden paths down the roads of their life, even if those roads are paved with ill-natured forces that have little to do with the destiny and potential of the travelers. Often, we settle for roads offered or put upon us rather than roads we have paved for ourselves.

The directions of our spirit are expressed in my conjure practices in the four points or roads that form the crossroads of spirit: life, death, luck, and love. Each one of these roads carve out specific expressions of our spirit into this world. They also embody the roads to happiness and fulfillment for us. When I discuss the gates into the spirit world and the ways of working with the Dark Rider at the Crossroads, who is the intersection and leveraging point of these powers, I will discuss them even further.

Managing your spirit-path requires an understanding of these other roads. What follows is a solid description of their scope and depth of power. This list is not exhaustive, but it gives a general direction for the spirit worker to review for inspiration on the goals of the spirit.

Life: This covers areas including health, childbirth, new goals, growth forward, road openings, vitality, inspiration, and increasing.

Death: This covers areas including physical death, endings, regeneration, road closing, finality, blocking, curse removal, blocking, and decreasing.

Luck: This covers the broad area of wellbeing. Luck is about being in alignment with your own inner spirit and addresses success, power, prosperity, prominence, and attraction of benefit.

Love: This covers areas of magnetism, attraction (romantic and other), marriage, fecundity, self-esteem and -worth, passion, and joy for life.

There is nothing that we want or need that does not somehow fall into these roads. The first time I ever heard of them was from an Appalachian root worker in West Virginia who said it probably came over from Africa with the slaves. The need for a relationship to what my mother called the good things in life is based on our relationship to our spirit, the Spirit, and these roads. When a client comes to me with a problem, it is always related to these roads. When a client comes to me with a desire, it is always related to these roads. So, relating to them as the roads of blessing or lack is a powerful way of governing the gifts of our spirit and its life in the embodied world. Our relationship to them can be any of the following states of being:

- They can be open with the fullness of their blessing flowing into our life.

  - *In this condition, clients will feel like they are greeting all the blessings from roads and just want protection or blessing work on them.*

- They can be blocked by something or someone in the way of the blessings.

  - *In this condition, clients may feel that the roads are not flowing and that they are in a condition of lack, suffering, or unease. They may report that they have been cursed, crossed, or are in a run of bad luck and may need to be cleared, covered, blessed, and protected.*

- They can be open and flowing, but the client has a particular goal in mind that is not being met.

  - *In this condition, clients may feel that their roads are flowing well, especially given the blessings they have received in the past. But they may want to ensure that a current goal or desire is in line with the roads.*

- They can be too open with too much activity.

  - *In this condition, clients may feel overwhelmed by the level of activity happening in their roads. They may want to slow the flow so they can have a chance to be at peace with their lives. There really is such a thing as too much of a good thing, and this condition embodies it.*

- They can be pinched, with minimal flow.

  - *In this condition, clients may feel like they get some success in certain roads but that it never amounts to much. They may feel that they are doomed to a meager existence and that is just what God wants for them.*

- They can be dormant or closed, never having been open.

  - *In this condition, clients feel like they have never been able to achieve satisfaction or blessing from one or more of their roads. They may feel like they are doomed to the fate of their family, and in fact they may have a road, say, to the prosperity of life and general wellbeing that is closed because their spirit has never lived around it.*

- They can have what I call speed bumps that seem to slow down or hinder their flow during certain transitions, traumas, or success points in one's life.

  - *In this condition, clients may feel they have minimal or even predicable levels of achievement in a road but that every time they hit a certain level, something or someone comes along to set them back. This can feel like a curse.*

My mother once gave me the following piece of wisdom: "To get something on you, you have to get something off you; and to get something off you, you got to get something on you." Though this may seem like a piece of trite country wisdom, it is profoundly instructive and wise. It basically means that if you want something, you have to get the blockages out of the way. For instance, if you want more monetary wealth in your life, you have to get poverty or lack of prosperity off you. And to get the poverty off you, you must start reaching to a prosperous spirit and get it onto and into your spirit or energetic field. In spirit doctoring, this occurs through what is commonly known as crossing and uncrossing. Now, in most books, crossing is seen as bad and uncrossing is seen as good, but use of these terms in this way is overgeneralized and inaccurate. I have seen these terms in Voodoo, hoodoo, Santeria, witchcraft, and conjure practitioner language, and with varied meanings. I will define them for the purposes of this book, but I do not suggest that these are *the* traditional meanings for them, as there does not seem to be any real consistent form.

Crossing and Uncrossing

Over the years, I have heard the terms *crossing* and *uncrossing* used in many ways. Traditionally, *crossing* has referred to hindrances, harmful influences, curses, ill-fated influences, and other terms describing a state/condition wherein a person is impeded from wellbeing or bonded to a harmful influence. When most workers use this term, they are referring to a harmful condition. However, I was taught that crossing literally refers to whatever is crossing your spirit-path (good or bad), including those influences we inherit or acquire from our family, culture, life experiences, self-development, intentional action, or projection by other people or forces. Likewise, *uncrossing* has referred to the removal of the crossed condition including cleansing, cutting, and clearing as well as removal of influences and conditions. The way I learned it was that *uncrossing* simply means to change a condition from one state to another; it refers to whatever needs change. It may also refer to a condition that is leaving you, and thus having you in an ambiguous condition until you are crossed by the next phase of life. One way to think of the intersection of these two conditions is that our lives and their expressions are like the weaving of a cord. As we weave in a cord for the intertwining of a braid, we must move another cord to accommodate it. Sometimes our life cords get knotted and we need to remove these knots, which may be done naturally as part of an ancestral paradox; be incurred by our intentional or unintentional design; or tied into the cord by trauma or the ill wishes of another that are cast into our cord by action, relationship, manipulation, or magical skills. It is the job of the conjurer to assist clients in assessing the nature of the negative or unwanted conditions that cross them, what they desire to cross them, what needs to be uncrossed from them, and whether spiritual forces are uncrossing (like fraying a cord) from them that may need to be rewoven into the cord. The worker seeks a strong life cord and a crossroads filled with a balance of life, death, luck, and love.

Spiritual Assessment and Reading

Just as it is important to notice any pains or unnatural/unwelcome changes in our physical health, it is also important to see this in the manifestation-power and inner feeling of our life states. By manifestation-power, I am referring to our ability to

- Have clarity of thinking and feeling to determine our desires, goals, and intentions in life;

- Maintain that clarity, enthusiasm (motivation), willpower, and energy to focus our actions on establishing the relationships, situations, resources, and other opportunities to achieve our goals;

- Maintain the flow of our lives toward the achievement of the goal; and

- Address and respond to any deterrents or other needs for addressing the direction, flow, and shape of our goal and its stages of achievement.

These are elements of what I call manifestation-power, and they are primary to everyone's ability to achieve their desires. When we have these elements in a strong level of flow and vitality, it seems that we have power. When we do not, we feel powerless. One of the goals of conjure is to increase our own power over the direction of our lives. Notice that clarity is at the top of this list. It is also important for us to consider that there may be a mental health or emotional disorder occurring. Spirit doctoring is not intended to replace or supplant these clinical interventions. However, for most people, this work helps immensely, even concurrent with clinical treatment.

After years of root-doctoring work experience, I have found that there are four ways the worker can get information to assess a person's spiritual condition:

1. The reports of the person affected;

2. The reports of family, friends, and other loved ones;

3. Observable symptoms; and

4. Information provided by some form of spirit reading, such as bone reading, card reading, palm reading, or use of pendulums.

As a support to our own root-doctoring work, I have included some examples of symptoms and possible scenarios that may indicate that an individual needs spiritual cleansing. The detailed list below is based on my observations and includes classic signs reported to me by my peers in conjure and witchcraft work.

• The reports of the people affected may include unexplainable and chronic confusion, headaches, insomnia, feeling depleted and unmotivated, an observation that the achievement of many of their life goals never seems successful and no prayers seem to work, anxiety, dread and heaviness, pressure between the shoulder blades, aching feet, swelling feet, pressure in the middle of the chest like weight is on it.

• The reports of loved ones may include an observation that the individual seems confused, non-characteristic of himself, like there are shadows around him, like he cannot hear what is offered by others, outbursts of tears and anger with no clear reason, an observed pattern that appears like life seems to block him from happiness, and that the loved ones feel pulled down by the individual's negative energy.

- Observable symptoms may include confusion; inability to focus; fear that someone is working magic on them; strange appearances of wounds, burns, or scars during the session; observable spirit activity around these clients; and an overexcited or pressured demeanor.

- Information provided by some form of spirit reading may show that these individuals are crossed by someone or something that is impeding their wellbeing. This might include bad inner patterns; negative relationships; family patterns; spiritual dilemmas that they must work through; some energy or spirit they have stepped into; an ill wish that has made its way into their mind or energetic field from someone else; or an invasive energy such as a ghost, curse, or other form of negative entity that is on or in them. The reading will also help with remedies and directions for assistance in growing the life roads of the person.

All of these means of assessment yield information that will guide the worker on the intensity and type of cleansing and clearing needed. These will tend to fall into three major areas: cleansing for a serious or ongoing (chronic) concern, which may be a seven-day working; general cleansing, which may be a one-time cleansing; and cleansing for new roads, which is focused on achieving a specific goal. If the concern being addressed has been a part of our lives for a long time, it may be deeply rooted and will require repeated cleansings of different types. This type of cleansing will get at the taproot of the problem and then work on the many hair roots that may be offshoots of it. As you can see, this work is indeed a doctoring process, except it is working at changing internal and external states by addressing the spiritual and spirit qualities of the people being cleaned and changing their lives at the most basic level and outward. In this way, it doctors the root of the problem instead of simply shaving or mowing off its surface.

Anyone who has gardened knows that problem plants (weeds) are often stimulated into more vigorous growth when you pull their tops off without pulling out the roots. There are multiple ways to do a cleansing. I will provide some of them in my description of a four-step method that I work with. It is not the only technique, but it is tried and true.

Four-Step Spiritual Cleansing and Clearing

There are two aspects of our spirit that lead to an embodied or manifested experience. One of them causes; the other draws experiences to us. Another way of looking at them is as one being electric (causing) and one being magnetic (drawing). An old granny woman told me that one part of our spirit sends out a call or casts a net, while the other hears the call and attracts or pulls in the net. In spiritual cleansing, both of these attributes of spirit must be cleansed—and they can be through this through this four-step method. It is important to understand that there are other conjuring methods for cleansing, such as lodestones, chicken feet (scratching from heel to toe), and Native American practices, such as the use of a sweat lodge. But this four-step method is one that is easy to do and very effective. The technique works like this:

Step 1: Water

Cleanse the physical body and the spirit forces closest to it with water that has been blessed and filled with a cleansing bath preparation. This bath is a mix of herbs, minerals such as salt, and solvents such as bluing detergent and vinegar. Always use an odd number of ingredients, and never more than nine in total. When doing clearing baths, you should always cleanse by cupping up the bath water and pouring it over your body, washing downward with a hand-sweep. Also, always step out of the bath backwards to leave the bad spirit forces behind you. Read more about this process in next chapter.

Step 2: Smoke

Cleanse the projecting spirit of your body by "smoking" yourself, also known in Native American traditions as smudging. Burn some form of herb in an abalone shell, incense burner, or metal or earthenware container. The preferred herbs include any of the following singularly or in combination: angelica root, white sage, lavender flowers, tobacco leaf, or coffee grounds. Be sure to sweep downward with a bird feather or wing or a Bible.

Step 3: Fire

Sweep your body with strokes moving downward with the flame of a lit white candle dressed (anointed) with hyssop oil or olive oil. This is called the sweep of light and places a cloak of light around and on you. Of course, you want to be careful of getting the flame too close to your skin or clothing.

Step 4: Covering

Nature abhors a vacuum. After cleaning out and filling with the power of holy light, you want to dress yourself against intrusions and bad spiritual forces. This stage is called covering because it covers you against the reentry of the forces you cleansed out, or others like them. I recommend the use of hyssop herb oil or tea. I have found the oil to be most powerful. The covering (also known as crowning) is done as follows:

Place a good amount of hyssop oil on your right index finger and anoint the back of your head where the spine joins the skull (the medulla region). Trace a line from that point across the top of your head to the front (the third eye area). Continue tracing a line from the third eye around the side of your right temple to the back, all the way around to the left temple, and back to the third eye area, making a circle. Continue your line of oil up to the soft or indented place in the middle of the top of your head and trace a sacred symbol, such as a Christian cross, six-pointed star, equal-armed cross, or five-pointed star. The combination of these points forms a crown of blessedness over you.

Anoint your elbows (both left and right). The anointing of your head and elbows forms an upright triangle, which my teachers call the eye of God. This both protects you and brings divine presence to your head—that which you reach for and which reaches to you.

How Does a Cleansing Feel?

You may wonder, how does it feel when you are cleansed? My clients and I have found that this way of working leaves you feeling relaxed, assured, lighter, less confused, comforted, empowered, and relieved. A cleansing and crowning unpacks the energetic baggage that is weighing you down. It allows room for us to energetically, spiritually, emotionally, and mentally breathe. It makes room for our spirit to bring forth more power to everyday life. I always recommend that after this four-stage process, you begin to pray or meditate to bring closer the qualities and virtues of spirit that you actually want to grow in your inner and outer life. There is nothing more comfortable than a clean home, whether that is your house or your body-house. With your body and spirit clean, we are ready to look at ways to fix your life with the spirit forces you want and deserve in your life.

Chapter 7

Fixing Yourself with Good Spirits

You get what you pray for, but do you even know your own prayers?

—JOHNNIE ROOSTER

This quote was shared with me when I was very young. I was told that it came from a root worker named Johnnie Rooster. I never met him in embodied life. He had been in the spirit world ("dead") for over one hundred years when his presence was given to me. You might say he was the first spirit contact passed to me by a spirit worker. My understanding is that he had experienced life both as a bound and a freed slave, as his life spanned the time before and after the Reformation. I heard many stories about Ole Johnnie. First I was told that he was born in Africa and brought to America in the slave ships in the early 1800s. Then I was told he was born in slave's quarters in Virginia in the same time period. These kinds of spirits are shared with their own kind of folklore and mythology. What I do know is that he was real when I felt him, and I can feel his power as I write this book. It is a common practice to have spirits passed to you as a part of your family in conjure working. Because of where I grew up and when I grew up (early '60s and '70s), I was lucky enough to learn from spirit workers who had powerful spirits and knowledge to pass on.

My understanding of this quote is that you need to appreciate the message you send out to God and the spirits—and *how* you send it out. It is sound, centuries-old wisdom, and all who live in the spirit would do well to live by it. I have found that many people have a sense of what they want in life, but their daily practices and mind-sets are contrary to what they say they want. For instance, they may claim that they want more money or other forms of prosperity, but they only speak of what they do not have. In my experience, if your lack occupies more time in your awareness than the growth of what you have, then you are on a one-way course to more of what you do not *say* you desire. Interestingly, we often become so comfortable with predictable pain and limitation that we forget how to move beyond it. We may say we want our lives to change, but we only talk about the current or past condition of our lives that bring us suffering. Often, we talk about our suffering as a way of getting attention and recognition, and we become the very story of what we say we don't want. This is what we must get off of our spirit to make room for—to attract the very spiritual forces and qualities we really want and deserve.

This chapter is focused on re-doctoring our root to grow strong and vital and to know the difference between sustaining stimulation and painful types. Once we can get the qualities and feelings of what we think we want into our daily lives, we can begin to court the principle forces that we *really* want.

First, we must cleanse ourselves of the old patterns of spirit. Then we realign our spirit with the forces we want to grow out from ourselves and the God we serve.

How Do We Send Signals to Spirit?

In earlier chapters, I discussed our relationship with our spirit and the Spirit. Now we need to take that concept further to discuss our relationship to the spirits of good fortune. By this I mean the inroads from the source of all spirits to our spirit and thusly, our embodied and expressed life. You see, in conjure, everything is a spirit. The world is alive and teeming with spirits and spiritual power, and the outcome of our lives is primarily dependent on our relationship with this inflow. The inflow is connected to the spirit roads of life, death, love, and luck, but now we will take the concept into specificity.

We send our signals into the spirit world in many ways:

- The words we use to describe lack, loss, and routine patterns;

- Our general attitude about ourselves and life

- The story we tell about ourselves, community, culture, generation, family, and so on;

- The content of our prayers, meaning whether we pray with a focus on what we don't have visibly present or for blessings to be increased; and

- The symbols and images we wear on our person or use to adorn our homes, cars, or places of employment.

This is only a partial list of the many ways we radiate our desires to the web of spirit. However, if we monitor and use discernment in how we send these signals, we can change our lives in miraculous ways.

There are many achievable and doable ways that conjure teaches to redirect the signals we send out to the spirit world towards a frequency or prayer that guides our life towards a direction of happiness, fulfillment, and wellbeing. The first step is to understand what we want in life and how we relate to what we want. If we always say that we will never be happy or have the good things in life, then that is the directive we are giving to our spirit and the spirits of good fortune. Through cleansing and clearing work, we can shed that ill-intentioned covering and foster a more fulfilling life with the roads of spirit. In my experience, there tend to be a few general spiritual forces that most clients want to reconnect with and grow into their lives, such as prosperity (money), health (physical and mental/emotional), love relationships (romantic, friendship, and familial), and general wellbeing and blessing (luck). After cleansing work to get the old spirits and, as my mother would say, dead prayer off us, we are ready to get a new prayer into our spirit. The focus of conjure at this point is to doctor the root of its wounds and draw blessing of good spirits into our life. A part of this is the understanding that all the things we want in life are connected to a stream of spiritual power also known as a spirit. This means that to get what we want, we have to open the stream to flow from our spirit and to our spirit. We do this by dressing ourselves, dressing our home, and fixing spirits of good fortune to ourselves and our homes.

Growing Your Spirit Through the Principle Forces

So how do we go about the practical aspects of growing the four principle forces of the crossroads and their specific inflows into our lives? Let's look at the principal spirit roads again.

Life: What do you want to grow in your life? What is your relationship to it now, and how is it fixed to your life?

Death: What do you want to end or cleanse yourself of? What will you have to let go of to get what you want, and are you ready to let it go?

Love: What do you want to court in your life? Are you courting your self? You may have to end your love affair with self-deprivation and isolation to make room for what really fulfills you in a person, place, or thing. How do you relate to your life? Your own life, your own spirit, is the first and primary relationship in your life. Once this relationship is strong, other romantic relationships begin to flow in a more healthy way.

Luck: How do you feel about fate? Do you feel that it is there to bless others but not you? Are you ready to make a new and positive relationship with this spirit?

Fear not—few, if any, of us have a solid relationship with all four of these roads. However, we can change that; knowing what we don't want is the beginning of getting what we do want. There are a number of ways that my conjure teaches us to re-relate to these forces, including altars, pots (specialized drawing altars), charm bags (also known as hands or mojos), anointing/covering/

fixing baths, and daily prayer or spell work. Please understand that old habits take time to break, and if the relationship you have with these forces has been established over a long period of time and even through multigenerational transmission (family or cultural curses), then they will take time to change.

Altars and Pots

The use of altars is a technique found in traditions all over the world. They are focal points and places for meeting God/the Spirit (the unified spirit), deities (specific embodiments of spirit), ancestral spirits, and other spirits for bringing about inner and outer alignment of self with these forces. Altars can be placed within our homes on tables and stands or may be present in nature or public places as focal points into the center of all existence through a specific spirit road. However, they are embodied—they are places where human spirit, the Spirit, and spirits meet to exchange and co-create something or some state in the inner/subtle or outer/expressive states of existence. They are places where the human spirit ascends, descends, or otherwise encounters spirits to work in the power of conjure. They may be devotional for exaltation of the spirit or a "working place" to engage in a creative way with the spirits. For people who have temples, I consider a temple to be an altar that you step into. A temple may have multiple altars or roads of spirit leading into and out of it as a sort of magical dancing floor for human and others to engage, encounter, exchange, and co-create. Altars can also be seen as the cockpit of a spiritual plane. Through the experience of the altar, the human participant navigates through the winds of spirit, carrying his or her desires to a destination. However you view it, the altar is neither the beginning nor the end of a spirit relationship. It is the middle place where the two levels of spirit meet and dance in an exchange of power and companionship.

There are many kinds of altars in spirit doctoring and conjure practices. Some are for devotion or praise to the spirit of the altar. They may be as simple as a table with items such as Bibles, Christian crosses, statues, offering bowls, flowers, candles, incense burners for offering sweet scents, rosaries, smudging implements, sacred pipes, or a host of other sacred or religious items. These types of altars are usually for encountering the sacred, though they may be used as working altars as well. A working altar is one in which the human encounters a specific powerful spirit such as God (or the holy family), archangels, personal spirits, or the principle forces for broad or specific work. All altars in conjure are places of respect and communion. In conjuring work, even if we have working altars, we consider the spirits that we work with to be a part of our family. We do not go to the altars or other working areas only to ask for help. We make offerings and prayers to them regardless of need. In fact, my partner and I light the candles on our altars daily with the intent of feeding the vitality of our spirits with the flame and lighting their way to our home as their home.

I will share with you a number of household and outside altars and meeting places of spirit to give you a sense of their breadth and scope in conjure practices. House shrines might include such forms as tables, vessels (containers), step-altars, doorways, or blessed windows. Some of these approaches may be very new for you, as they are specific to the spirit practices of my culture. A vessel is a specific container such as a pot, bucket, tub, or jar that is used as the honoring or working space, usually with a personal spirit or principle force. For instance, the spirit of Chief Blackhawk requires a bucket or tub to define his space. Everything that sets in that bucket belongs to him—his pipe, hatchet, flag, knife, and bust image among them. Another spirit I work with, La Madama, is a Congo spirit who was also a conjurer and likes to be put in an iron cauldron. There are also other spirits in the principle forces that like their own pot too, such as the money spirit.

A favorite of mine is the step-altar. This form of altar works by drawing power down from the supreme source, the Maker, to the working, or conversely stepping up an existing condition and returning it to the Maker to be un-made. The form I was taught consists of a three-level altar like three stairs of a stairway. The top stair upholds the power of God, the Maker, the Source, the Great Spirit, or whatever concept the worker projects through to reach contact with the creator of life. The color of the candle placed there is white for the color of starlight. The next stair down is to Jesus, the man (woman) God, or what I call the touchpoint of human and divine. The color of the candle is red for blood and power. The last step down is for the work, the worker, or the condition being addressed. The candle color is black for rich earth, magnetic/holding power, absorption, and mystery. For clarity, in conjure black is not wicked or evil. No color or attribute is. All colors and powers can be used for help or harm, and magic should never be blamed for the intentions of its worker.

The step-altar way of working can be seen as a waterfall of power that flows down from the heart of God into the heart of humanity, earth, and/or manifestation. It can also be seen as a detangling and disintegration of a form or pattern from physicality or the heart. In spirit work, the worker's focus may be making (drawing, attracting, creating, or growing) or it may be un-making (repelling, sending away, destructing, regenerating, or dissolving), and the step-altar allows the worker to work with these modes or currents of spirit. Once a step-altar is constructed, the worker uses it to do work or for devotional reverence. Some workers also put statues, crosses, iconography, prayers, and other items on the steps to touch the level of God being reached for at that step. As you can see, there are many ways of inviting spirit into your life through conjure.

One principal force that we all deal with is prosperity. Prosperity can come in many forms such as money, gifts, full health, and many other means. However, our relationship to it allows the fruition of life's gifts to flow into our lives. Money, like magic, is not responsible for its use or abuse. This particular form of prosperity is representative of our currency symbolizing prosperity and is often a source of stress that affects other areas of this principal force, such as fertility, health, stability, and so on. It is for these energetic relationships that I always recommend workers to re-bless prosperity and dismiss poverty and lack from their own spirit. A very fun and powerful way of doing this is through the construction of a money pot, which could also be termed a prosperity spirit. Next, I will provide you with the technique as my teachers shared it with me.

A Recipe for Attracting Prosperous Spirits

My teachers shared this technique for constructing a money pot with me. I don't know anyone who can't use more prosperity in their life!

1. Get copper and tin bowl. The ones I grew up around were often lard cans or other kinds of tin cans, though

the combination of copper and tin metal have the most power to draw this spirit and its influences.

2. Get a large lodestone. A lodestone is a chunk of iron ore that has magnetic qualities. I usually like one the size of your fist. This allows room for both feeding of the stone and setting a small statue on it.

3. Clean your bowl and lodestone by washing them in living water. Living water is water running in a stream such as a creek or river. You want the stream running away from you to take any bad energy out of the bowl and stone. Run both of them through the smoke of burning tobacco and white sage. Then sweep them across the flame of a candle that you have blessed.

4. Take the lodestone up to your mouth and tap on it three times with your fist or pointing finger like you are knocking on a door. You are knocking at the door of form to open the house of spirit. When you do this, say, "Awaken unto life . . . I honor you, spirit of the lodestone . . . remember your power."

5. Put the lodestone in a triangle of blessed white vigil candles for the night so that it can feed off the power in the candle flames. It is always good to offer food to a new guest and soon-to-be tenant in your home.

6. Put the lodestone in the pot and place the pot so it is facing your front door. After all, you want money and other forms of prosperity to come into your door and live with you.

7. Now we come to the phase of this work where you have to gather your money road (an aspect of the luck road)

to you and your pot. Basically you are assembling the body of your prosperity spirit, and the loadstone will help you with its magnetic drawing power. This stage involves finding hunting money and teaching it how to hunt for you.

8. Hunting money is money that you train to hunt for other money. When you are out in your daily life and find coinage or dollar bills in your path, it can become hunting money. If the head of the coin is up, simply pick it up and say in its ear, "Hunting money, you found me and welcome home." If the coin is face down, then acknowledge that by saying, "Oh, hunting money, you are lost and I will help you find home." Turn it over once in your direction, saying, "Hunting money," as you do; do it again and say the same thing; then do it once more (three times in total). By the third turn, the coin will be facing upward. Say, "Oh hunting money, you found me." Take it home and put it in your money pot. This is called laying a money track, and it is setting a road for money to flow toward you. I was also told that this is seed money that grows other money. In fact, when my pot starts filling up with coins, I like to use that magical money to buy candles, lodestone food (iron filings), Hoyt's cologne, and other items to feed the pot.

9. When you find dollar bills or decide to put some in the pot, speak into the ear of the president pictured on the bill. Welcome him to your home. Roll the bill toward you into a scroll—that is the direction through which you want the money to flow. Rolling the bill toward yourself is like a beckoning finger saying, "Hey

you, come over here," or rolling out the red carpet for the money spirit to tread in your direction. Place the rolled dollar upright in your money pot of coins so that the top of the dollar scroll is facing up. This is the mouth of your money singing heavenward to God. I always dress the lips of the scroll with some kind of magnetic oil or money-drawing oil. You can purchase these at conjure or hoodoo suppliers, botanicas, or New Age-type shops.

10. From time to time, feed your lodestone with iron filings to thank it for its work. Splash some Hoyt's cologne on it to dress it to go out into the world to work for you. I also put nine different kinds of dry beans in the pot, including fava beans, lima beans, kidney beans, and peas. Keep a rue-scented candle burning either in the pot or by its side to feed it more power and to protect your money. You can buy these at New Age-type stores or at an international grocery store that caters to the Latino community. They are often called "ruta candles" and have rue herb oils in them.

11. Lastly, get either a green Buddha statue or a three-legged money toad statue and set this on top of your loadstone. Both of these can be purchased anywhere that has feng shui or Buddhist statues and charms.

If you work the money pot by feeding and growing it, you will see considerable improvements in your income. This type of working is an example of how you create roads for a spirit to find you, welcome it to your home, and then praise and feed it to keep it strong. Remember, this spirit will become a permanent part of your family, and the money pot will extend its power into many other areas of physical prosperity, such as health. Though it is called a money pot, it is also a prosperity vessel.

Outdoor Areas for Spirit Doctoring

In this kind of work, everything and every place has magic and thus can be worked for the benefit of all. But let me tell you about some examples of outdoor working areas or shrines specific to spirit doctoring:

- Prayer rocks, which are large stones where prayers are written with chalk;

- Spirit trees, where people leave centerpost prayers or petitions (either by the tree, buried under it, or placed on the branches);

- Crosses and obelisks;

- Old tree stumps for throwing objects such as eggs for take-down energy;

- Stoops, stairways, and doorways leading into your house for dressing with washes, signs, and oils to draw principle forces and other spirits into or away from the home and its occupants.

Windows and doorways are excellent places to fix spirit forces to your home. Do this through prayer or by consecrating them and you will draw good spirits and repel bad ones.

Establishing an Altar

I have developed some steps for developing an altar or indoor working area for conjure practices. These steps are stages of a process that I have developed over years of working this kind of magic. I have not seen them in print anywhere else, but I have found them tucked away in the practices of my teachers and other competent workers I know or have met in my practices.

Step 1: Placement

Decide where you want to place your altar in your home. Will you put it high up on a shelf to oversee your house? Will you place it in your kitchen where nourishment is made or in your living room to invite the spirit to be a living part of your life? Will you place it somewhere where it faces your front door to both guard and shape the forces that flow into your life? Or do you want it at your east-facing window to fix your power to the rising sun and its power to regenerate and grow life? The concept of place really embodies the most important stage in the creation of an altar because deciding to do this is about making and holding space in your life for the personal and traditional spirits and the principal forces of conjure.

Step 2: Thinning

This step involves the way that we draw the presence of spirit from the un-manifest state to the edge of our awareness. We do that by sending our voice past the veil of form into the web of spiritual forces through prayer, fasting on the day we begin our work, or reaching out to the spirit world in the intention of companionship and co-creation. I think of thinning as the formal declaration to the spirit world that you are inviting it to come forward and bringing yourself to its door. I always recommend that workers take a cleansing bath, and I give a potent recipe for that later.

Step 3: Consecrating

Whether we are calling on the personal or traditional spirits or the principal forces, altar work and all conjure is working with the preconditioned, pre-formed creation power. It is working with creation from the inside out. For this reason it is imperative that spirit workers always bless and consecrate the thinning and relationship establishment aspect of their work. This forms the very nature of an ongoing relationship, and in my view, it keeps it clean, sacred, powerful, and contacted in the healthiest way. You see, we can call to these forces without consecration, and they will come. However, they will come through the shape of our own consciousness and the deep intention that called them forth. Many times we are filled with fear, longing, pain, anger, vengefulness, and a host of other states of consciousness that can set an inward road to our lives for the most invasive and parasitic aspects of the spirit world. Consecration helps us maintain our own spirit cleanly and clearly, so that the call that goes out from us to the spirit world gets answered by powerful but pure spirit beings. There are three components to the consecration: consecrate yourself, consecrate your home, and consecrate your altar. Below I provide you with recipes for all three of these consecratory components.

Consecrate Yourself

Consecrate yourself by doing the four-step cleansing process described in chapter 6 using this water/bath recipe: Mix 3 tablespoons sea salt, 1/4 cup vinegar, a few squirts of lemon juice, 3 tablespoons Hoyt's cologne, 3 tablespoons Florida Water cologne, 1 cup strong black liquid coffee, and 2 tablespoons Mrs. Stewart's Liquid Bluing with 1 gallon water and put it in jug. This cleansing bath fluid will be blue and smell very delightful. Now, this fluid is not to be consumed internally and, if you have allergies to scents or detergents, you will want to test your reaction to it. Take a cup of the liquid bath and put it in your bathtub. Then take a cleansing bath by pouring the water on your body and stroking downward to remove all negativity and curses while saying something like, "In the name of the Father, Son, and Holy Ghost, I release all wickedness, illness, and harm conjured by me, to me, or stepped in by me." Another prayer you can use came to me through my cultural tradition and goes like this:

> *Water wash the ill away.*
> *Water wash it gone.*
> *As the darkness gives away;*
> *Comes the rising sun.*
> *Water, water, water, water;*
> *Water wash it gone.*
> *Water, water, water, water;*
> *Water wash it gone.*

Then step out of the tub backward, drawing a large "X" in the air between yourself and the tub to close the road between you and what was cleansed off. If you can, take a cupful of the water and throw it at the setting sun to fix your work to the take-down power of the setting sun. Always cover yourself after a bath. I use hyssop oil to cover myself by putting a drop on my crown and a drop on my left and right elbows. You can also use the crowning technique I provided in chapter 6.

Consecrate Your Home

Consecrate your home by cleansing it physically and spiritually. Remember that your home is like a molding and holding force that wraps itself around you when you eat, relax, sleep, and go about your daily life. It is one of your most important and powerful tools. You must set its spirit so that it serves you and your family and does not keep you entrenched and entangled in a nonproductive or harmful pattern. I recommend a house cleansing that uses a similar approach to the four-step cleansing of your self. First, do an actual physical cleansing of your home. Bless some water by praying over it, or speak over it, saying, "Water, awaken unto life and remember your power. I honor you. Remember your power to cleanse and release it to me I pray." Then get some sea salt and speak over it, saying, "Salt, awaken unto life and remember your power. I honor you; remember your power to cleanse and preserve sustenance and release it to me I pray." Mix the salt into the water and stir three times, saying, "Be you pure as the first waters of life." Then take this mixture and walk through your home, dipping your fingers into it and sprinkling it to cast away all ill will, negativity, and harm while stating, "Be thou pure and exalted as the true spirit." Walk through your house burning a mixture of tobacco and white sage to fumigate your home with the cleansing breath. Then walk through with a lit white candle that you have anointed with olive oil to give it the sweep of light. Lastly, anoint the front door with a blessing oil such as hyssop in the name of the Maker by whatever name you use. I also like to anoint my windowsills and back door if feasible.

Consecrate the Altar

Consecrate the altar by doing the same process as above. Pray that the divine spirit work through this altar and bar all evil forces from it. Then ask God to send down his or her power into the altar and to the spirit you are consecrating it for. Anoint the altar with three crosses, side by side, unless you are working in another spiritual tradition. If so, use the symbol of spiritual truth and power from that tradition. Seal the blessing of the spirit on and into the altar. I like to then reach my feeling to the presence of spirit and feel the power flow into the altar, into me, into the spirit of the altar, and into the relationship between myself and the work of the altar. Some workers repeat the Lord's Prayer over it as well. The way I was taught to reach for the power of God to use in healing, blessing, or consecration is to anoint my palms with olive oil, turn the palms upward, and look to the heavens while saying, "God, I pray, incline thine ear unto me. Let the Mana fall, Lord, let the Mana fall." When the power comes into your hands, you can transfer it into the altar or wherever and however you need it to work.

Step 4: Feeding

When you invite Spirit or spiritual power to ascend or descend into your altar or vessel, you have invited a power to make its home in your home. Like all beings, these forces need to be fed or they will leave. One way of feeding the altar and the power it brings is with a candle flame. The spirits can use the fire from the flame to grow in their vitality. I light candles on my altar every day simply to light the way for my spirits; this welcomes them into our home and strengthens their power. I also offer coffee and provide a glass of water with honey or sugar in it. Some spirits like specific meals or flowers, and I give those when I am asking for specific work to be done or on the spirit's sacred day. I always advise my workers to do this for their spirits; if they do, many blessings will come forward.

Step 5: Engaging

It is generally considered rude to invite someone to your home and then leave them sitting alone. Daily practices, such as feeding the spirits' flame, will keep them strong, but engaging them in an exchange or continued acknowledgement of presence will take the relationship to the next level. I talk to my spirits a lot. I pray the blessings of the spirit for them, and summon goodness and strength for them. Sometimes I sit in my working area and feel their presence and talk to them; other times I just be with them. I thank them for their friendship, blessings, and presence in my life. Bottom line: I engage with them and their lives and their world.

Step 6: Working

If you have done steps one through five, then the relationship between you as the spirit worker and your spirits has begun to grow, and you are ready for a working to become a working relationship. At this stage you can begin to ask the spirits for help. Remember to make an offering in exchange for the spirit's strength when you ask for help. I put tobacco in a saucer and then put the spirit's candle on top of that so that the flame pulls up the power from the tobacco and feeds the spirit. Once the work is done and the goal is achieved, I give further offerings of food, rum, whiskey, an egg, or other items specific to the spirit. The list for these payments is too long for this book, but the reader can research the appropriate foods and offerings for each spirit. One thing I never offer is human blood—mine or anyone else's. I was taught that this is evil and dangerous, and I am keeping with the tradition as I was taught it.

Now that we have an understanding of how to manage our spirit and the spirit roads, we are ready to work the human spirits that live on the other side of form, known as the ancestors. Ultimately, it is because of the ancestors that all of us in bodies exist. Yet this form of work is often demonized, distanced, or just plain overlooked in contemporary magical and spiritual practices. The information I have given thus far will equip you with many ways to grow, know, heal, and reveal your spirit and ready you for direct work with the ancestors and their wisdom and power.

Chapter 8

Ancestral Spirits and Graveyard Magic

You cannot be a spirit worker until death "sets" on your shoulders and informs you.

—Ms. Granny

I had this teaching passed down to me long after Ms. Granny had passed into the spirit world. As a child it made no sense to me. As a young adult it made no sense to me. It has taken me nearly fifty years of life to finally understand it. It took facing the destruction of many of my inner illusions and the challenges of facing my own eventual death before I came to an understanding of its deep and genuine wisdom. I have distilled this wisdom down to three major ways that death informs us:

- The ending of our physical form is a backdrop of finite time that reminds us to live well and fully now;

- The spirit world beyond the embodied "living" one is vaster and older than the form world, and thus it is an unfathomably deep well of wisdom and power; and

- The concept of death puts more value on our life force right now as opposed to later (there may be no later).

Once we look into the face of our mortality, we can get about the process of empowered and conscious living. When we face that power, the forces on the other side of the veil of form can begin to teach us in wise and powerful ways that help us avoid the mistakes they have made or the ones we may yet make.

When we bring our attention to the touch-point of awareness where the seeming singularity of our current life touches a deep ancestral stream, then the shelf life of our body's world does not bind us; it sets us free. At that touch-point of spirit and inner-knowing, we meet one of the most personal threshold beings of our lives. Daddy Death governs the inflowing tide of life we erroneously call the end of life. I have found that what he really teaches is the end of lies. He is the spirit through which we enter back into the fullness of the web of life and into a waking state of living where we know ourselves as living in a larger stream of spiritual presence that is always available. Therefore, a goal of the conjurer is to die before we die. This means to embrace and co-create with the ancestral current of life before we enter into it through the end of our current physical life. The first threshold of experience and understanding of this is embracing death as an illusion.

Death Is an Illusion

There is no doubt that the death of our form or the form of someone we love is traumatizing, and it calls our attention to the moving tides of this thing we call life. This thing seems to have two tides: a tide that flows out into the form world, and then one that draws back into the seemingly formless world. All of our embodied lives, we have been taught how to communicate, relate, take on roles, perform tasks, and even play in the world of our embodied experience, or what I call the outflowing tide. This does have great value for integrating into our species, but it leaves us ill-equipped for co-creation and communal life with the rest of the world's life-forms in the seen and unseen tides of life. We are basically taught that this embodied experience *is* life, and therefore it ends with our physical death. We are taught that we must fear the other side of life. Often, we are taught to relate to our physicality as though it is *all* of our life, but this is not true for the person who is both alive in spirit as well as alive in flesh. In truth, until we are alive in our spirit, we are only partially alive in our flesh.

Our religions and spiritual practices teach that there is an afterlife, often expressed as being the place of rewards (heaven) or the place of punishment (hell or something like it). Honestly, as I have grown my spirit, I have come to believe that it is doubtful that God or Source is so petty as to punish us with everlasting damnation for our choices. This may offend some, but it is my truth. We have been taught in our religious practice that we either need to get out of this life and into some form of heaven, or that death is a final ending to something and a beginning into a place we cannot know until we get there. These approaches can be damaging to our spirit, because they make us afraid that either the passions of our embodied life may cost us our eternal one or death is a force that is going to make us stay somewhere, good or bad, depending on whether God likes our choices. To the spirit worker, we do not have to wait until death to know the blessings of the inflowing tide. Through our direct encounters with this tide and the ancestral beings that live in it, we can go from blind faith to informed faith based in direct experience and inner-knowing. This is the ultimate meaning of the concept of dying before you die: you discover that this life is not our only chance and that the range of living extends to and through embodied and disembodied states of life. In fact, in working with the otherworld, we begin to know that we are already alive in the spirit world, and we have a large community on that side of life.

Once we can overcome the fear of the transition between living states, both sides of this veil open their blessings to us. Once we anchor our heart, the very thing that pumps both the inflowing and outflowing tides of life, we can navigate the full spectrum of life. Now, are there spirits in the ancestral world that are unclean, dangerous, and unwholesome? Yes! But then, are there spirits who live in flesh that are murderers, thieves, rapists, and other dangerous people? Yes! This is why we must always endeavor to cultivate our discernment by living our lives consciously on the whole flowing tide of life. This is why cleansings, coverings, altars, prayer, and so on have been emphatically stressed in this book, and in many other spiritual doctrines and practices worldwide. If we enforce those practices in our daily lives the same way we practice good relationships, communication, boundaries and goal setting, prioritization, common sense, manners, and self-governance in our embodied lives, then we are on the right track. *This work is very much about reclamation and sovereignty of your spirit—your whole spirit in the whole of the life tide.* To me, dismissing the inflowing tide as the end of life, as opposed to a very sacred aspect of life, is a great step in that direction.

No Wisdom Leaves the World

Another wonderful teaching in conjure is that no wisdom leaves the world. This means that all of the knowledge and distilled experience of all the embodied life that has occurred on the earth is still in the earth's memory and in the river of humanized spirit that streams out through us. We only have to redirect our awareness into that level of life and it will guide us. There is an immense wellspring of insight, wisdom, and power waiting for us in this deep well of ancestral wisdom. For the record, we are not talking about making the dead come back to life or preventing souls from moving on, whatever that means. I have found that the soul does not move away from the rest of spirit, but it does (if it is regenerate and healed of its pain) move into a powerful, peaceful, and reconciled state of being without paradox and entanglements. By entering the wholeness of spirit, the soul of humanity is synchronized with a deeper, richer, and more profound level of life than words can ever express. I believe this may be the heaven that we are told about. This heaven is not gained by conforming to some dictate. It is accessed by purification of our spirit and unifying it with the wholeness embodied in the word *universe*, which etymologically means one ("unus") song ("versus"). How beautiful it is to understand our lives as parts of one great dance or "turning."

Another aspect of the no-wisdom-leaves-the-world teaching is that the soil remembers. My teachers were adamant that as we disintegrate our physical selves into the soil of the planet, it retains a distilled fractal of our memory. Over time the rain, snow, and passages of the circle of earth's rhythms leech out the memories of suffering and disconnection, regenerating the memory into a form that is useful and nourishing to the earth. For some this takes time, and this is why we sometimes feel a field of sadness around particular graves. In fact, on occasion, if my inner spirit or God says it is right, I will do a cleansing at that grave to help either the residual memory to heal or the soul of the interred to find wellbeing. I was taught that the root worker is not only supposed to work for healing and helpfulness to persons on this side of the tide, but the for the inflowing one as well. I have found healing the disembodied spirits and their residue in this world to be incredibly fulfilling and rewarding. In fact, it has strengthened my spirit and increased my spiritual and magical skills to levels I never could have dreamed. Spirit workers can access the power of the memory left in the earth through buying graveyard dirt for conjure work. But before we move into the mechanics of that practice, let me introduce you to Daddy Death.

Death Is a Gateway State and a Spirit

Another one of the wise conjure wisdoms passed on to me was the concept that death is not an event, it is a person. The name of this person in my tradition is Daddy Death. Upon first glance, you may think that death as a person is the silliest thing you have ever heard. But if you understand that a part of doctoring the root is knowing where all causal forces originate in the oneness of eternal being, then all things are persons—not just humans. The stretch in understanding for a lot of people is in embracing the centrality of consciousness and the intelligence or sentience within all types and states of life, including the inflowing tide. I feel that one of the flaws in modern science is that it fails to include the element of intelligence, which the spirit worker knows as spirits of the one force called God or the Maker, within and guiding all processes. Without this concept, there is no way for us to communicate and connect with the spirit within events, things, people, places, etc. Healing this disconnect brings humanity to a peaceful place with life instead of an illusion of isolation that fuels chronic terror and the many symptoms that grow out from it.

Once we can imagine that death is a gateway state out of the embodied experience into a broader one that is more awakened, life expands its very aliveness to us. This thing called death is a state of being that we pass through; its feeling will depend on the contents of our inner landscape, also known as imagination. If I imagine that death is a lifeless biochemical process, then that is what the web of spirit will grant me as I exit. If I imagine that the gates of death are lined with fearful demons out to snatch and harm me on the way out, I will experience that. If, however, I know death as a friend, a person who serves the oneness and vitality of life, then that is what I will encounter as I exit. So I advise conjure workers to die while they are alive and to know death as a gateway spirit and a wise friend that will let us pass in and out of his spiritual dimensions while embodied. Death will lead us into healing and wellbeing on our exit on the outflowing tide.

Approaching the intelligence of Daddy Death or the event of the death will lead us away from its frightening foreignness and into its familial presence. The concept of Daddy Death in my conjure teachings likely came from Africa, though it may have European influences too. His image shows up in Africa as Papa Guédé, in Europe as the Grim Reaper, and in the Middle East as beings like Azrael, the angel of death. He has been seen by many as a person who comes and gathers us when it is time to leave this world. In my experience, he is a person who always lives at that place where we exhale our breath, with hope that we can inhale the next one. He guards his children buried in the graveyards, for these bodies are his treasure trove of wisdom. He is the guardian of the spiritual dimensions of the graveyard and the guide to the gifts it has to offer. He is an invaluable threshold teacher in the work of spirit doctoring and a dear and precious friend when we take our step into his realms. The best level to understand is the spiritual dimensions of his home on earth and the power of the threshold into that realm.

The Spiritual Dimensions of the Graveyard

On the surface, a graveyard appears as mounds of soil with bodies beneath—gravestones and tombs with writings and epitaphs about the birth and death dates, names and some characteristics of the lifeless body buried there. But when we shift our awareness into the deeper and more spiritual dimensions of the place, these things mark the name of a book lying beneath, radiating its knowledge and experience. To open this book, we need only move into a spirit level of exchange by entering through the centerpost spirit known to the spirit worker as Daddy Death. In short, how we enter the graveyard will determine where we enter. Are we simply visiting decomposing bodies interred at a place for visiting fading memories and feelings of loss? Or are we visiting the radiating life that these bodies continue to have, within the soil and foundations of the earth? We can visit either one, and I often visit both, for they both have value depending on what we (the embodied) seek and what they (the interred) need. But it all depends on how we enter this yard.

If we want to enter past the death of the yard into the inner life of the yard, we have to enter through the keyhole into that world: Daddy Death. We do this by purifying ourselves with a cleansing bath before entering, or at least anointing ourselves with hyssop or olive oil. This ritual has a twofold worth. First, it blesses us against the intrusion of any parasitic spirits or painful memory imprints still lingering around the graves. Second, it prepares us to enter in a sacred and spiritually powerful way. I also recommend that you cleanse yourself in a bath, anoint with Florida Water, or reach up to the Mana of God to wash you after you leave, just as a matter of energetic hygiene. The years have been overlaid with such an expectation of sorrow that there may be residue.

The process of entering in through Daddy Death works like this:

1. Knock at the post to the right of the entrance to the graveyard three times, stating to Daddy Death why you have come and asking for him to open the way into the spiritual dimensions of the yard.

2. Leave some type of offering such as tobacco or rum to honor and feed him.

3. Wait for his answer. You will feel that you are invited or dismissed in your inner feeling. Honestly, I have never felt him say no to me.

4. Enter with respect and reverence—no sorrow or sadness. If you get drawn to a grave to hear a spirit tell its story or to weep for its passing, then do it until it feels like it is draining your energy in any way. If this happens, wish the spirit well, call Mana to clean you, and move on.

5. When you are done working in the spiritual dimensions of the yard, come back to the entry point. Walk out backwards to prevent spirits from following you home. When you are back at the gate, knock three times at the post again and thank Daddy Death for allowing you to enter. Tell him you will visit him again.

This simple technique has profound power. The first time my students perform it they are impressed with the feeling and vibrancy of the graveyard while they are within its spiritual dimensions. They also report that it seems smaller, more intimate, and definitely alive and even holy. Now, to develop your relationship with a specific grave or graveyard further, you have to enter in through grace.

Entering Through Grace

To enter the yard through grace is to make your relationship foundation one of ca. e, compassion, respect, reciprocity, and power. I was taught by my conjure teachers that seeking the "conja" or spirit power is best done through a graceful spirit. This invites the spirit of your work to come forward in a collaborative and familial way. This is not to say that you will never encounter harmful spirits, for indeed you will. Again, this is why discernment of the spirit is so stressed in this book. In most cases, if you reach to the spirit of your work in a respectful and caring way, it will reach back with the same kind of spiritual quality. There are "hot" spirits that are less graceful, but kind in their own way. They are akin to the schoolteacher many of us had who seemed mean but really cared about us and wanted us to succeed through competence, discipline, and strength. Occasionally you will work with spirits (ancestral or other types) that are tricky and deceptive. Again, this is why you use discernment, discipline, the covering of a higher power, and your own divination tools to ask if this spirit is of beneficial intent. I prefer to use pendulums and coins as what I call discernment tools. Making offerings at the entry into the yard to Daddy Death is the most powerful step towards a relationship of balanced grace and power.

Another very powerful way of entering in through grace is what Mom called washing the stones. In my culture, this is often done on Memorial Day, which we call Decoration Day. What we did back home was get a bucket of water and put a little sugar or honey in it. Then we'd take a rag washcloth or sponge and literally wash the gravestones of our beloved family or friends. Now, this fluid is quite sticky and can attract insects, especially ants and flies. I was told these insects would take away the sorrow of the dead as they ate and drank the fluid. When it was done on Decoration Day, the focus was on veterans of war, but the spirit workers would do it other times too. As a witch and conjure worker, I love to do it on All Hallow's Eve (October 31) or All Saint's Day (November 1) for respect and honor.

These days I like to use Florida Water cologne and/or Kananga Water cologne in my washing fluid. The Florida Water has great power for cleansing, blessing, and attracting good spirits. The Kananga Water brings good fortune and is used as an offering to ancestral spirits. I do this practice with graves I work with often. I also like to do it throughout the graveyard where I do a lot of conjure work. The feeling I hold and declaration I make to the yard is for each gravestone I cleanse to clean all the gravestones there. And may this sweet wash remind all spirits interred or living there of the sweetness of life and of spirit. I wash the graves after doing the entry work with Daddy Death I taught you previously so that I am working not just in the "flesh" of the yard, but in its "soul."

Another very powerful way to enter into the grace of the yard is to pray for the dead. This is even more powerful when we do not personally know the person in the grave, but are drawn to it in the spirit of grace itself. Now, I often pray for my ancestors wherever I am, in a graveyard or not. Having this as a regular part of your practice will greatly strengthen both your relationship to your ancestors and the power and wisdom they give you. It does not call any spirit back from where it is living now, but we must understand that our spirits are much bigger than a specific place and time. It is a vast web of being in its own right and we can pluck that thread through a grave, through our love, through our prayers, or through a host of other techniques. When we pray for the ancestors, we are dipping the spirit web through our grace and power and moving the blessing force to the person of that prayer. When this is done with no intent beyond the wellbeing of the ancestor, there is a ripple effect that has immeasurable healing affects on the ancestor, the person praying, and the totality of humanity. Praying without a focus on ourselves expands the power of our spirit and brings holy power into all of the realms of existence.

I often get questions from students and clients about what ancestral spirit(s) might want or need. Because they are not in physical form, their needs are of the spirit. Here is a short list of suggested qualities for you to use in your prayers to carry from the throne of spirit to the heart of the ancestors:

- Peace

- Comfort

- Rest

- Healing of sorrow

- Strength

- Knowledge of their sacredness

- Union with the divine

- Safe passage

- Knowledge that they are loved

These attributes of the blessing power are needed by all beings, human and other, embodied and ancestral. Perhaps the times we suddenly feel an unexplainable joy, peace, or strength come into our spirit while we are "alive" are actually someone in another time visiting our grave, praying for us. When you feel that, just say thanks to God and pray a blessing for the ancestors and whoever or whatever just prayed for you.

Tending the Graves of the Forgotten Dead and the Unknown

Two final techniques of grace that I will provide are tending the graves of the forgotten dead and laying flowers upon the graves of the unknown. The first technique is about finding old graves that are neglected and clearly forgotten. My experience is that most graves over a century old either have no family alive to remember them, or the family does not know or care about the grave. What you do is to kind of adopt the grave. Begin visiting it and talking to the spirit of the interred person. Use the person's name. You may find that you are called to the grave and that you get a tingle or some sensation when you are near it. That could be because the spirit or memory of the person recognizes your spirit, sees you as a spirit worker, and notices that you have the ability to experience their presence; in more rare cases, it might very well be one of your bodies from another life that is buried there. I recommend that you wash the grave, pray for the spirit of the person there, and tend the grave, including offering flowers, flags, or other decorations. If the birthday is marked on the grave, it is a powerful gesture to bring flowers, share a glass of wine (drink a glass and leave a paper cup of some on the grave), or do some other form of celebration. You can even visit on your birthday. If there is any wisdom or power left in the grave or the soil around it, those attributes may begin to flow to you as a gift of reciprocity. I have also found that these graves become a powerful place to buy graveyard dirt to work with. The other technique of laying flowers is a form of respect for the spirits associated with the graves and Daddy Death himself. It simply involves getting cut stems of flowers and placing them on as many graves as possible. Clearly, the smaller the graveyard, the more graves you can honor. I like to announce to Daddy Death at the entry to the yard that I am coming to honor him and the graves in his care. I find this practice strengthens my relationship with him and it feels very good to all the spirits (mine and the grave's) as an act of grace that opens and grows the spiritual qualities of compassion in my heart.

Buying Graveyard Dirt

One of the most traditional forms of graveyard work in southern conjure is working with graveyard dirt, sometimes called goufer, goofer, or goofa dirt. I have also heard it called boneyard dust. It works on the concept that the earth is filled with memory and that soil is where it is stored. In this work, you are working to buy power or wisdom from the memory that has been radiated by the deceased body into the soil around it. What we know and the power we have continues to be remembered by our body, even if the soul has left and moved on. This power radiates into the soil and lies dormant until it is awakened and summoned forth. We are not buying the soul of the person. For instance, if I have a friend who is a powerful nurse for children while she is alive in her body, when she dies, her body will still radiate that power and wisdom, so I will want to go to her grave and buy dirt when I am concerned about the wellbeing of a child's health. However, we still may go to any grave to ask for help; if it has power and is willing to help, you can still get power. If you know there is a lawyer or judge buried in that grave and you need help with a law case, then you have specialty power right there.

When we buy dirt, we do not desecrate the grave in any way. That is illegal and unethical, and I do not condone it. We are buying a few spoonfuls of the soil, not a shovel or more. This work is the very opposite of disrespect and disregard of the dead. It is founded in the facts that graveyards are old places of wisdom and power and that the dead body is a reservoir of these attributes. It is also founded in the notion that the body is not buried to be forgotten, shelved away, or treated as a disgusting corpse or icon of sorrow. The body is a transmitter of spirit and a holy book that has only been shelved, not cast away. The older the grave, the more powerfully radiated the soil around it is. I have watched this work change people's lives in front of me as they realize the sacred power of the grave-yard for not only meditation and reflection but also contin-ued magic and empowerment of life. It just has to be engaged, summoned, cared for, honored, and directed—but only in the spirit of spirit doctoring and absolute respect, not morose fear.

Sometimes you will encounter what my mom called a live grave, which is very powerful and animated, and may even have the soul of the deceased still visiting it. You will know because you will feel the power and presence of the grave very strongly in chill bumps, heat or cold waves on your skin, audi-ble messages, or sudden emotions flowing through you that are not your own. This can be either a bonus or a burden to a spirit worker. If it is simply a powerful and animated grave, then you may have a source of power presenting itself to be employed. I advise that you use discernment to determine this. However, if it is an actual soul that visits or is staying at the grave, then you need to see if it is suffering or wants or needs help. You find this out through the use of the same kind of tool. You may need to hear the story of the soul, pray for it, cleanse its grave, or give attention to its healing for a while. If you find that your energy is being drained, then bid it farewell, leave the graveyard, and take a cleansing bath. Unless you are skilled as a healer of the dead, you may not have the technol-ogy to help. Next, I will give you an entry-to-exit technique for southern graveyard spirit work with gathering and buying graveyard dirt.

Supplies to take to the graveyard:

- Crown Royal whiskey, light rum, coffee, and/or tobacco

- Three new pennies or buffalo head nickels

- Tobacco (if the grave is of a Native American)

- A zip-top bag

- A spoon or trowel

- A paper cup

Step 1

Use the entrance technique honoring Daddy Death that I have already provided, but also ask him if you may enter into the spiritual dimensions of the graveyard to gather dirt. Tell him why you need it. Wait for an answer. If you feel yes, go in. If you feel no, don't. If your feelings are too subtle in your perception yet, then use a tool for discernment.

Step 2

Go to a grave you have been working with (or ask Daddy Death to lead you to one that can work with your needs), a grave you have already identified, or use some form of dowsing such as rods or a pendulum to find either a live grave or one that both has the power to give you and is willing to help. There are traditional techniques that I learned from my mother, but I cannot give them in a book. You will have to see me in person to learn that information.

Step 3

Once you have identified the grave, tell the spirit of the grave what you need and ask it to help. Test to see what the answer is by using your inner sense or a tool of discernment. Then, once you have determined the answer to be affirmative, collect the dirt. The area to collect the dirt is based on your estimation and the purpose. Here is a general guide:

Head: Education, learning, clearheadedness, increased perception, memory, clarity, changing someone's opinion or judgment, knowledge.

Heart: Love, heart ailments, compassion, emotional need, friendship. This is also a general area for all purposes when in doubt or for general healing.

Groin: Impotence, fecundity, pregnancy (desires or prevention), power, sexual potency.

Left Hand: Attract money, establish friendship, call something or someone back from a distance, get a new job or promotion.

Right Hand: Domination, power, gain new acquaintances, make things move forward, power over a situation or person, defense.

Left Foot: Buy a home, get someone to move with you, let go of the past, uncover a secret.

Right Foot: Move forward, leave a relationship, leave a job, get stagnation and atrophy to change. (The right hand helps with this too.)

This list will give you a sense of areas to collect the dirt from, but as you do this work, more insights on technique will come to you. Just let your spirit, the Spirit, and God speak to you. Daddy Death will also lead you through your intuition to other powers granted through the areas of dirt collection.

Step 4

Once you have collected your dirt, you must thank the spirit for its wisdom and power. Then, in the area where you spooned up the dirt, place the three pennies in a triangle around the area with the heads of President Lincoln face down to draw power to the grave and its spirit power. Then place your paper cup in the hole and fill it with the rum, whiskey, or coffee. Take a drink from the bottle for yourself and share this toast together. Leave this offering and any other you have brought. If you can, come back another day to retrieve and discard the offering cup as a sign of respect and trash cleanup.

Step 5

Go back to the entrance to the graveyard and walk out backward so no spirits follow you home. Reach over to the pole where you knocked three times entering. Thank Daddy Death and ask him to let the way be closed until you come again. I always leave another offering of tobacco for him, or sometimes I spray rum from my mouth onto the post or entryway to give it more power. I also like to sprinkle some Florida Water cologne over the entryway so that the path into the yard is always blessed. Then either at the entrance to the yard or when I get home, I wash my hands with Florida Water and do the cleansing bath to make sure I did not pick up any sorrow along the way.

You may wonder how you use the dirt once you have it. You should take it home, dry it out, add a pinch of coffee grounds or cayenne pepper to give it more power, let it sit for a while in the center of a triangle of white vigil candles to fire it up, and maybe sprinkle a little rum on it for more life. Then you can put it in a red flannel charm bag alone or with an odd number of herbs, stones, or other items that are specific to your needs. Using the mojo-making technique I will share in chapter 10, tie it closed using three knots, and then put it to work. You can carry this charm or put it near the area or person you are seeking to influence. You may need to tell the bag who it will be working for or on so it knows the direction to use its power in. If you are carrying the charm bag or have made it for someone else, I recommend that it be placed in a triangle of white candles every now and again to keep it strong. Maybe even sprinkle three drops of Kananga Water cologne on it to feed the spirit of the bag.

The Centerpost Practices of the Graveyard

Another aspect of working in the graveyard comes out of the centerpost practices of conjure. This concept is a core element in my tradition. The concept of centerpost work is that the center of creation is wherever you place your eyes, though the circumference cannot be seen, but only felt. The centerpost can also be seen as a specific door or even keyhole into the spirit world, and it shapes the way power flows into and out of it. In a way, each of us are centerposts through which a specific aspect of the universe flows, and around which a series of relationships comes together to the emergence of our form into this world. *We are source, centered into the substance of our being.* Therefore, each of us is a center through which and out of which universality expresses itself; this centerpost has expanded (stellar and heavenly) aspects, deep (inner/underworld and ancestral) aspects, and elemental or form-based aspects. Thus, the centerpost (just like the sacred tree of witchcraft) has three levels of its being. When we direct our attention to a grave or tombstone, it becomes a centerpost into the tripartite power of the spirit within it. When we knock at the gate or post upon entering the graveyard, it becomes a centerpost through which we enter into communion with the flow from the center of existence we see as Daddy Death or the ancestral current of life and spirit. Sometimes in conjure we knock three times on a centerpost such as Daddy Death's gate, or even on the roots we work with in mojo or the centerpost within the graveyard to open the center of the post with a call for it to be a gateway.

Once we have entered into a graveyard's spiritual dimensions through Daddy Death, we can find yet another centerpost through which to enter into the guardian and guide of that particular graveyard. It will either be the tallest cross, tallest obelisk, or oldest tree in the graveyard. Occasionally these will actually be situated at the physical center of the yard. This monument can be a centerpost into the whole inner network of spirit power in that graveyard. When I work in this way, I first present myself to the post, and then I feed it rum by spraying it out of my mouth onto it. This feeds its power and shares essence between you. Then I knock on it three times while saying, "Awaken unto life, guardian and centerpost spirit. I honor your power." If you feel the power come forward from it or if your tools of discernment indicate that the guardian has welcomed you, then you can work with it. You can ask the spirit to show you the right grave to work with. Or you can write petitions for problems to be worked on and bury them at its base. This spirit has access to all the wisdom and power in the yard. When you are done, thank the spirit, ask the way to be closed until you knock again, and leave some form of offering such as tobacco or unused coffee grounds.

Ancestral Altars

I don't know any old-style or traditional root workers, conjure doctors, spirit workers, or spirit doctors who do not have an ancestral altar, a vessel called the soul pot, or some other form of honoring and engagement work with them. In fact, my teachers would think it was disrespectful at a minimum and downright ridiculous to be doing any work in the spirit world without honoring the roads of your blood and spirit. After all, no one gets into this world but through ancestral blood. We are each carried into this world on it through our mothers, and we are carried back out of it at death by our breath. Our ancestral spirits of our blood and of our adoptions and other relationships are interwoven into the tapestry of our destiny. I am not just referring to the ones we have known in this lifetime but also to the ones we do not know directly who nevertheless live in our blood and touch our spirit. When no other spirit hears us, they do. They have a direct investment in our life walk of clearing ancestral paradox, bringing our power to the blood, revealing our power into this world, and continuing our blood or spirit lines. In a way, they are living through us as we will live through others when we pass beyond the veil of form. They are our closest spiritual next of kin, and they cannot and will not be ignored. It is so easy to reach to them because they are already reaching to us. There are a few techniques for doing this in my spirit practices, including: saying daily prayers and honoring, creating ancestral altars, doing gravesite work, and creating soul pots. I will provide some simple instructions for each one of these techniques. I advise all workers to do as many of them as possible. The ancestors are not only holy, but they are also powerful. They can strengthen our work or become a hindrance to it. They want to give us their love and support, but we must invite that to us through sound spirit practices.

Daily Prayers and Honoring

Daily prayers and honoring techniques can include all of those already listed, or they can be simple prayers that we do for our ancestors individually or collectively. In prayer work, it is always good to thank our ancestors for their lives, without which we would not be. I enter into prayer every morning and, often, many times through the day to maintain dialogue with my spirit, God (or the Mother Spirit, as I call it), and the spirits I work with as well as those of my blood and spirit. The ones of spirit are the ones I have been adopted by in initiatory traditions, friendship, and other ways. I may look at the list of qualities I have already provided you; or I may simply look to my heart for what blessings to call to them. Other honoring techniques that I use include observing their birthdays, attending their gravesites, and reflecting upon their memory and spirit with love and gratitude in quiet moments throughout the day.

Ancestral Shrines

Ancestral shrines are a dedicated memorial place or meeting place for you and the memory, spirit, power, and blessings of the ancestral spirits. These shrines can be as simple as a small table, the top of a bookshelf, the top of a dresser, or other simple and practical areas in the home. I was told that they should be in places where the ancestors feel welcome and a part of the household and family. There are no hard-and-fast rules to the creation of these shrines. In fact, most of my folks never even called them shrines or altars. They would just say that a certain wall of pictures or tabletop with pictures plus a place where they could leave things was their family table, memory wall, or memorial. The ones who were doing active spirit work would say, "This is my family and where I keep showin' 'em that I love 'em and ask for their help." If you use a wall of photographs and drawings, it can be useful to have a shelf or tabletop in front of it for offerings. I was told it is important to have pictures, personal items (jewelry, hats, smoking pipes, etc.) because they are actual likenesses of the ancestors or have their energy in them. A vase of flowers can also be very useful, as the spirits can use the life force from them, especially if the type of flower meant something to them while in form. You can also offer glasses of fresh water, because water feeds the soul and brings back memory of aliveness. I also spray favorite perfumes or burn incense. Offering of a flame from a candle is very powerful because the spirits use the power of the fire as life and light force. They can feed on this to sustain their link to this world. Or, as a worker once told me, it lights their way through grief's shadows. These structural components and simple offerings are ways to honor and strengthen these spirits and invite them into your life.

Gravesite Work

Gravesite work has already been covered to a degree. However, in this particular aspect of it, you are not necessarily buying dirt but simply honoring the body's final home in this world. Attending graves on holidays such as Christmas, Easter, birthdays, and other important dates (that may vary in religious and other traditions) is another powerful way of demonstrating honor to the ancestors. Decorating their graves with flowers, wreaths, or statues, and even leaving small stones or three pennies on the gravestone are simple but effective ways of honoring and keeping their memory and spirit healthy and vital. Throughout my childhood, my mother and I would visit her brother's, father's, and mother's graves every Saturday around dusk throughout spring, summer, and fall. We would place flowers, sing to them, and clean their gravesites. I could always feel the strong power of their presence, and somehow I knew they would always protect and bless us because of this simple magical practice.

Soul Pots

The use of soul pots is a very old-style approach that I learned from a Southern Appalachian worker in my community. I also saw soul pots in other workers' homes when I was growing up. These vessels are a container, home, and meeting place for the aggregate spirit of our ancestry. They are also a form of center-post like the one in the graveyard, except they are specific to our personal ancestry and are placed in our homes. I was told that the practice came from Africa with the slaves and found its way into the practices of other races, including whites, who were poor and marginalized. I have written and taught about this technique in many places because it is powerful, old, and sacred. I gave detailed instructions for making the soul pot in my book *The Tree of Enchantment*, but I offer them here again because the soul pot is so central in my understanding of conjure work.

1. First, find a vessel that has a top that either screws on or can be secured when it is moved. I prefer metal or earthenware urns. Whatever you choose, make sure it is pleasing to you. If you want to make a pot for friends and others who are not connected to you by blood heritage but are considered family, simply make another pot for them. You can have as many pots as you can attend to.

2. Next, identify the graveyard and graves of your familial dead from which you would like to buy dirt. You will want to visit as many sites as possible.

3. Upon entry into the graveyard, use the entry practices I have already provided to you, including knocking at the gate, to honor Daddy Death and enter into the spiritual dimensions of the yard. Wait for a moment. If you feel welcomed, state why you have come (your intention).

4. Find the grave of the person you are seeking.

5. Reach your senses into the presence of the person buried there. Sense whether he or she approves of your collecting soil from the grave and if he or she is willing to assist in your life.

6. Once you get an affirmative answer, estimate the area of the grave where the heart of the person may be.

7. Dig a few spoonfuls or even a small cupful, depending on the size of your soul pot. Be mindful that you must not be destructive in any way. Many graveyards do not sanction this practice.

8. Place a small biodegradable paper cup or shot glass filled with whiskey or rum as an offering. Although alcohol is the most traditional offering, if you are concerned about this person having an aversion to alcohol, then offer tobacco, coffee, or some other food or beverage that is pleasing to that person.

Now you can exit the graveyard the same way you would if buying dirt. Take the dirt you have bought and put it in your soul pot. As I stated in *The Tree of Enchantment*:

The process of collecting soil for the pot occurs over years. The soil stays in the pot. Upon the death of its owner, it can be dumped in any graveyard where an ancestor is buried. It can also be passed down to someone else. On a consistent basis, you should make offerings to the pot by placing such things as food, beverages, liquor, or coffee on plates or in cups before it. The essence will be used by the accumulated spirit of the pot within twenty-four hours. After that time, the offering should be disposed of in the trash, down the toilet, or otherwise discarded. It is important to place a candle before the pot and light it as a bridge for the spirits to cross.

The vessel becomes a central part of the ancestral altar and the dwelling place for the spirit of the ancestor (aggregate spirit). When you need assistance, light the candle, call out to the ancestors for their help, state the request, and make an offering once the request has been granted.

This soul pot should become the very center of your ancestral altar, especially if is going to be used as a centerpost for your conjure work with spirits of the dead. These pots can become very powerful and are highly cherished by workers serving them.

Discernment Tools

The last area of teaching I will share on working with ancestral spirits is what I call discernment tools. Let's face it: none of us has crystal-clear subtle/inner senses every day. Sometimes we are just too stressed, tired, or out of sync with our sense of whether the spirits want us to work with them or whether they are the right spirits to work with. Over the years of work in this practice, I have come to know that there are many reasons that we may want confirmation for our inner senses. I use two primary discernment tools to confirm or secure my initial answers: the pendulum and/or a technique of tossing four Mercury-head silver dimes.

The pendulum is an object that can be dangled loosely from a cord, thread, or chain. I have worked with several types, including pendulums already made and given to me (that can also be purchased at stores, online, etc.) and those made by tying angelica or an old skeleton-style key to a red cord or other string. You want it to be able to dangle loosely. One old style I learned as a child was using an old key on a string and a Bible. We would hold the key by the other end of the string and then, with our eyes closed, dangle the key over whatever page we opened the Bible to and let it drop. We would then read where it dropped as instructions related to our query. In the graveyards, I usually just use the key or angelica root style and ask questions for a yes/no answer. When you first get or make your pendulum, it is useful to wash it with Florida Water cologne, tap on it three times, and ask it to awaken unto life and then ask God to put power and truth into it to cover it with blessings. Ask it for a *yes* and see what direction it turns, then ask it for a *no* and note the same. This will let you know how the language of your pendulum is spoken from your own inner spirit. Proceed to use it in the graveyard or any time you need an answer working with a spirit or on a situation or condition. When it is not in use, store it in a sacred way, because it is a treasure partner in your work.

The Mercury-head-dime-tossing technique works by taking four of these dimes, praying over them, asking a yes/no question, and then tossing them to determine the answer. Mercury dimes were minted in America between the years 1916 and 1945. They have a winged face of liberty on them, but they look so much like the Roman God Mercury that they became known as Mercury head dimes. They are much coveted by conjure and hoodoo workers because Mercury is akin to the opener of the way or the crossroads spirit that is so prominent in both the African and European magical practices. These coins are also 90 percent pure silver, and silver is used in a lot of our magic.

The technique involves getting four of these dimes, preferably minted in a leap year (1916, 1920, 1924, 1928, 1932, 1936, 1940, or 1944). Clean the dimes and pray over them the same way you did with the pendulum. When you have a question, ask God to speak through the toss, ask the question, and toss the coins. The more dimes that land heads up, the more the answer is *yes*. The more tails that show up, the more the answer is *no*. If there are at least three coins heads up, I take it as a solid yes. If there are four heads up, I take that as a definite yes. If it is fifty-fifty, I may ask further questions, go to another grave, change my approach, or work on another day and see what the answer looks like.

As you can see, work with ancestral spirits and graveyard work is a deep, sacred, and powerful well of inspiration. The areas of work I have provided for you coupled with what you have already learned and developed through the previous chapter will create a solid foundation in ancestral conjure that is in line with the old-style ways.

Chapter 9

Gates into the
Spirit World and Encountering
the Dark Rider

*Half the work of gettin' the power is in gettin' yourself
through the door of the haints.*

— Anonymous Root Woman

This quote was shared with me several years ago by an
African-American root woman I met in Washington, D.C.
She was known in her community as a powerful faith healer,
spiritual advisor, and spirit worker but was not public in any
way. I was blessed that she even spoke to me—she knew that
I am both a witch and a public figure in the conjure world.
Her words rang with such truth in my ears because they were
raw, real, and direct. What she was saying was that a large part
of the effort that spirit workers must do to get at the power
of conjure is to get themselves beyond the everyday way we
see the world and into a place where we are in the presence of

God and the spirits, to leverage that power or blessing from the haints (Haunts or spirits) into this world for the purpose of a happy life. The door is perhaps the most important part because it embodies the principle of the threshold. The threshold is where we as humans both meet the otherworld of spirit and come onto the dance floor of this magical practice.

There is much preparation and internal work that we must do to get through that door, navigate our journey while moving beyond it, manage the power that comes from and through it, and be able to close the door without locking it when we are done with our work. Indeed, we live in a physical form and must never allow ourselves to be lulled into the nonphysical world in such a way that we lose our anchoring here. When it is our time to wholly live in the discarnate world, we will do that. But for now, and while in bodies, as spirit workers we want to have a foot in both worlds, navigating each with equal value. This is what the threshold work of conjure requires of us. It requires the ability to doctor the root of those who live on both sides of the door in service to God, the spirit, of all three of these realms of life. We have really delved into means to declare sovereignty over our own spirit in this world and the other. We have looked at how to grow the spirits that work with and through our own spirit, including those ancestral spirits that live on the inflowing tide of life. Now, we can look at working with the threshold spirit, the holy throne, the light of God, and lastly, the root powers of the mojo or spirit bag. By entering into this work by working with our spirit, the Spirit, and the ancestral spirits, we are better equipped and more spiritually mature and able to work with expanded powers and additional direct ones.

The Door of Spirit and the Throne of God

The first time I ever heard of this threshold level of our spirit, it was called a rapture state, and then later the throne or door. The elders would often rock back and forth, usually at church in the pews or on their front porch in rocking chairs while praying, until they were called into what they felt was the presence of God. They called this state of being "a rapture" because they were being called up to God, the Maker, into a rapture with the power that made the universe. They would speak of this as being called up to the throne of "Ole Maker" where they could speak in his ear or be given his blessing on their work. I experienced this many times when prayer, praise, or the rocking (or quaking as it was also called) drove me into an altered state. I would sometimes be incoherent, either speaking in tongues or what seemed like gibberish, but this is called the spirit tongue. As I have grown as both a witch and a spirit worker, I have come to realize that this was a trance, but I think it is that and so much more! My experience is that it is an actual opening between the human spirit and the spirit world. It is a change in perception, a change in spiritual presence, and an encounter with spirit beings that are alive, powerful, and often just beyond the reach of our everyday senses.

This door can be drawn closer to our consciousness by techniques designed to reach for it. We may use prayer, chanting, repeated charms, psychotropic drugs and alcohol (which are more dangerous), simple rites, and conjurations. This chapter is about taking what we have been working with in the previous chapters and adding some simple and powerful ways to work with threshold power. We have already worked with it in the ancestral realms with the gatepost at the entry of the graveyard (the door of Daddy Death) and the center-post in the graveyard. The use of pots, such as the money pot and the soul pot, are also examples of centerposts and thresholds. These are thresholds into the human and human-focused levels of the spirit. The next levels of threshold work are with nonhuman beings connected to principle forces (the roads of spirit and good fortune) and the power of conjure itself.

Tapping and Knocking

Tapping and knocking is perhaps the simplest and also the most easily dismissed aspect of the ways I was taught to conjure. It is both about tapping the root (the spirit) and opening the threshold between humanity and the rest of the spirit world. This form involves knocking three times on a grave, tapping on a root, or knocking at the center of the crossroads or other thresholds to open the way or road into and out of the vast realms of the spirit. When we work with the root of a plant, a stone, or the meeting place between ourselves and God, the Dark Rider, Daddy Death, and a host of other spirits, we announce ourselves and our intent, and then we signal for the illusionary partition between the realms of existence to part themselves. This signal is the knock or tap. It is also a way that we humans connect with the spirit world by touch-meeting at the perceived interconnection point between seen and unseen. It is a way of announcing our presence, requesting a relationship, and bringing about an opening in the realms of perception and experience. It has many symbolic meanings that were shared with me by my conjuring and witchcraft teachers, and I will share a few of them here.

- It is the gate to heaven approached by knocking at the door of the Father, Son, and Holy Ghost.

- It is a gate to the three worlds of stone, sea, and star.

- It opens the way between the ancestors, humanity, and heavenly hosts.

- It calls the three aspects of existence to come forward as one.

- It opens the gates of heaven, hell, and this world.

Ultimately, I think all of these interpretations are correct. I know that when my students and I knock three times, we feel a presence come forward out of us, through us, and to us, and perhaps these are truly the three realms of our lives. When we knock, it is as if we as humans are finally saying, "No, the way can be opened and we will no longer dwell on the outside of life" or "We are presenting ourselves to the rest of the spirit world as a neighbor, co-creator, and companion in creation." When I knock, I feel it first in my body, then in my heart or soul, and then in my spirit. When each of these three feeling areas comes together, there is no doubt that I am in rapture and oneness with the source through a relationship with the specific spirit or spirit road at the door.

Have you ever knocked at the door of a long lost friend, a dear family member, or someone you dearly want to meet, and when he or she opened the door you felt the rush of excitement, joy, power, oneness, connection, and even attraction?

This is the feeling that the root worker feels when he knocks on the door and feels himself tapping the spirit from the center of his being to the center of the other being—a meeting on the dance floor of creation. Without this feeling, the power of the work does not come forward. Remember that the conjurer conjures power and spirit out. The root worker reaches from his root to the root within a person, place, or thing in concert with God, the root of all creation. These are all different terms for the southern tradition workers doing the same thing, entering as a spirit to the spirit or spirits of their work. One of the most prevalent ways of doing this in conjure is through candle work, also known as setting lights. This is one of the easiest and most direct ways of experiencing that connection, because what we feel as life feels warm, and fire transmits this power.

Entering Through Fire

I did not hear much about candle work in setting lights until I moved to the big city. Folks did not have a lot of money to buy candles when I was growing up, and there were no real candle stores around anyway. We did not have candle shops and botanicas in Winchester, Virginia, or the surrounding areas in the 1960s, 1970s, and early 1980s. But I did hear of some practices using hearth flames, bonfires, and the like for conjuring spirits, setting payers into the hands of spirit, or calling forth the blessing power. What I will share with you I learned from workers in the metropolitan area of Washington, D.C., and Maryland, and later from southern workers in Alabama, Georgia, North and South Carolina, Mississippi, and Louisiana. These folks were simple but powerful in their approach to working with candles and their flames as a tool for entering the threshold of spirit and leveraging power into blessings for the success of themselves, their clients, and their families.

One must understand that where the power lies with candle work in conjure is not in the candle color, though when color is added, the power of the candle work increases considerably. The power in this work is first in the prayer placed into the wax, because wax absorbs; second, in the power of the flame, because all fire partakes of the nature of God as the first starlight that lit the rest of the flames of life; and third, in the oils, herbs, Psalm dust, nails, pins, saliva, and other personal items and powerful forces used to load and doctor the drawing or repelling power of the candle being set. In old-fashioned work, tallow, beeswax, or plain white candles were all they had to work with. It is truly a convenience that we can affordably purchase candles of different colors and color combinations now, but that was not the case when I was learning this way of working. This luxury was not always available to old-time workers.

A very important part of working with candles is loading them. The loading is the point in the preparation when the power is being gathered into the gateway of spirit that is provided by the candle. There are myriad materials that can be loaded into it. In the old days, the herbs, stones, and other items were often harvested by the worker from the garden or the woods. Most, if not all, of the recipes were passed down orally from other workers or even from the parents of the workers, but today there are some fine root workers who have published books that I recommend as a reference for what to load into your candles. There are two books in particular that I recommend as compendiums for items to be either used to load candles or as prayers to use in setting lights: *Hoodoo Herb and Root Magic* by Catherine Yronwode (Lucky Mojo Curio Company, 2002), and *Old-Style Conjure Candle Burning* by Starr (*www.oldstyleconjure.com*, 2011). They are invaluable sources for traditional and old forms of loading candles and for materials for mojos, incenses, and so on.

There are many ways to load the candle, to prepare it for the light of the Maker to come down and bring it to life so it can radiate and draw power to create or destroy. Loading a candle with your items and prayers will imbue it with power. Items you could include are:

- Herb pieces and dust that have power related to the work you are doing (be mindful that twigs, flowers, and leaves can catch on fire);

- Psalms from the Bible, which are relevant to the work, that are burnt to dust and sprinkled in the wax;

- Nails or pins to hold in a charge or are stuck into the side of the candle to mark the days for burning;

- Rings, an earring, or other nonburnable personal items;

- Saliva.

Most modern workers do not put their saliva on the candle they have loaded and fixed for a client. They may do this if they are setting candles at their own home, or they may advise the client to do so at his or her home. Saliva work involves conjurers or clients praying hard until they feel the power grow, and then they spit the prayer-filled saliva into their hands and anoint the candle. This was the first and oldest way of dressing a candle that I learned, but scented oils are also very powerful and can be added to this work. More power is always good.

If the candle is dressed with oil mixed especially for the purpose or olive oil to bring it to its sacred and powerful vibration, it should be prayed on as a tool in the work. Oil has a unique way of connecting blessing powers and intent to whatever it touches when it has been spoken to. This is why it is used to anoint objects and persons in spiritual and magical rituals, as it connects each person into a unity of purpose. One way of doing that is to speak your intent, prayer, or desire directly to the oil while it is on your fingers or hands; call down the power of God into the oil; and then anoint the candle from the top (wick end) to the bottom to draw influences or from the bottom to the top to repel or uncross a condition. This will magnify the power of your candle, and, as my teachers said, will help it sing. Then there is the power that unites it with the will of God and the power of the living spirit. This power is transmitted through the flame.

I have already discussed many of the qualities of the flame that are like that of the living spirit that warms and animates our body and gives it what we see as life. Fire really has the power to stir our spirits and bring them to another place that is powerful, magical, mystical, and in the presence of God. Its presence is as an outpouring from the very heart of creation when we see it rise as the sun or descend from the heavens as lightning, or when it heats our homes, protecting us from the killing chill of frost. These attributes make it a formidable force for our spirits. Its personality is very much like our spirits—it is animated, hot, pulsing, illuminative, transforming, moving, and many other qualities that are aligned with our spirit. Its presence ignites change and transformation, and it is a mighty sword against the forces of darkness. Therefore, when we lift the light of our tapers to the heavens to merge with the down-flowing power of God, we are making a sacred circuit of power that has a lineage to spirit workers since the age of Egypt and before. When we honor the flame and call to it to remember the sun, the stars, and the heat of life, it transmits a pulse that gives life and transformation to all it touches. Therefore, when we light the magical candles and set the light of God into action, we call the blessings and power of God through the conduit of the flame and the memory of the candle to ignite its life into or out of this world, depending on the work at hand. This is enough contemplative material for you to use to tap into the gateway powers of fire and the setting of lights.

There are other places that are gateways of spirit where we can meet the spirit world in our conjurations. One such place involves water—specifically rivers and streams. Work with rivers and streams was a focal part of the spirit work of the Shenandoah Valley. I did not understand this for many years, but now I think it is related to the African tribes that were imported into Virginia. It is my understanding that many people were brought to Virginia from the Yoruba and Ibo tribes of Nigeria, and they brought with them the magic and teachings of Oshun, the Orisha of love and magic. This is where I believe they come from. However, I do know that this work was passed on through oral tradition, and that is how I received it. I leave its historic origins for academics to decipher.

River Magic

I was taught that rivers and streams are powerful gateways into the spirit world. Both of these waterways are what we call "live water," and they are used for baptisms (not only Christian ones), conjuration of new roads, and in-spiriting objects such spirit bags. For the spirit worker, these waterways carry spirit power to and away from us. I was never taught to use ocean tides the same way, but then, I was raised in a mountainous area in a valley hundreds of miles from the ocean, so that type of working would not have been a part of the folk magic of the geographic area of my youth. I was told that there is a powerful river spirit that we simply called the Lady of the River. She gives and takes life depending on the direction we face in her flow, and there are powerful forces that flow in her stream that can be worked with. Before you start working with a particular stream, I recommend that you do the following: find a small creek or river that is shallow enough to walk through with no danger of harm to yourself, present yourself to the Lady of that stream, and offer honey (pour it in) to sweeten her waters. Then use a discernment tool to assess whether she is willing to work with you. Once you have established an answer of yes or have found a stream where the Lady agrees to work with you, then you can do the following work:

1. Decide what you wish to work on or receive in your life.

2. Identify some of the forces or situations that are blocking your progress and that need to be removed. Do not think of specific people to remove. Rather, if a relationship needs to go away, think of and feel the presence of this entanglement.

3. Ask the Lady of the stream to remove this blockage by detangling and loosening it from your life.

4. Step into the stream with your arms crossed over your chest with the oncoming flow of the water streaming toward your back. Then, when you are in the center of the stream, open your arms and let the water flowing away from you take this influence away. If this influence has caused you pain or was once meaningful, you are likely to start crying. If this occurs, give your tears to the Lady, as this adds to the power of the work.

5. When you feel like it has been detangled and taken away, then, with your arms at your side, walk to the other side of the stream while thanking the Lady of the stream.

6. Once on the other side, contemplate what state or condition you wish to receive in place of the one you released.

7. Then, step back into stream. When you are in the middle, face the oncoming current, reach with your arms open as if to embrace your new goal or state of being, and ask the Lady for this.

8. Once you feel the new blessing flow into you, close your arms in an embrace around it and receive it.

9. Walk to the side of the stream where your work began, feeling a deep sense of gratitude to the Lady of the stream. Look for one stone to take with you to remember this power.

10. Pour some milk into the stream for the Lady's life-giving power to grow. Then leave and let the power work.

This form of conjure is elegantly simple, direct, and powerful, and it should not be underestimated. My understanding is that it is quite old.

One other form of river work that I have learned is to baptize, or "in-spirit," spirit bags, statues, medallions, and other magical items with the living water of the stream. Once again, we can see the connection between rivers, creeks, streams, and magic or the movement of spirit power. In this form, if the item is blessed to take something away, such as keeping evil or wicked workings away from the wearer, face in the direction of the water moving away from you and ask God to fill the stream with its power and to give the Lady the power to protect and take away. Ask the Lady to receive and grant this power to the item. Once you feel the power flowing, simply reach into the water that is flowing away from you and sprinkle three drops on the item. I was taught to say, "In the name of the Father, Son, and Holy Ghost," but you can seal this work however you like. If the item being blessed is to bring something to the user of the item, then face the oncoming flow of the stream and do all of the same steps I provided above. When you are done with your work, always pray that God, the Maker, or Spirit bless this stream and her Lady with all the goodness of life. This concludes our work with this very powerful feminine form of threshold work.

The last and final threshold working I will provide in this section of the book is one of the most potent I know—working with the Threshold Guardian of the roads of life called the Dark Rider at the Crossroads. He is a male form of threshold presence, similar to Daddy Death but for a different intersection of spirit.

The Dark Rider at the Crossroads

Of all the threshold spirits in southern spirit work, the spirit of the crossroads is perhaps both the most famous and the most maligned. Yet he is also the most alluring, intriguing, and foreboding. He is known to many as the Devil at the Crossroads, given fame by the great blues singer Robert Johnson of the late 1930s. Whatever Johnson encountered, whether it was an unpleasant agreement, a source of inner guilt, or just a very good story for selling records, the power of his image of the crossroads spirit has haunted the American mind for nearly three quarters of a century. His lyrics speak of going down to the crossroads and falling down on his knees, begging for mercy. Regardless of whether Johnson was speaking allegorically or whether he went to a crossroads in Mississippi for some kind of help from the spirit there, these words are gripping. They have some of the same elements I associate with the Dark Rider, such as: going to an intersection of roads where the spirit lives; asking God for power, protection, or to open the roads, though these lyrics may infer remorse to God; and the notion that other folks either cannot see him or recognize him because he is in the world of the spirits.

The concept of the Devil at the Crossroads is a familiar theme in both southern spirit work and the old-line witchcraft I learned. However, at least for conjure, I suspect that people used this name out of mere curiosity about this powerful spirit; to keep its power for themselves; or to illustrate the fact that the Dark Rider will make you face your own inner lies and adversaries within, so it's best to look inside one's spirit before frivolously seeking him. When I heard about him, I was told that he was not evil but rather very old and powerful and that he came from either Africa or Europe. I think he came from both places.

There is a lot of information in the name the Dark Rider. First, he is dark, or at least made out of the power of the night. This suggests that he is an in-between spirit who can only be encountered when light and night dance under the shadow of the moon. Second, he is a rider, or in movement, which indicates that his power and spirit nature is change. I have found both of these elements to be true. My mother first told me about him. I asked if he was really a dark man on a dark horse, and she shared these attributes with me:

- You feel a chill to your bones when he arrives.

- You may hear what sounds like the hooves of horses on the road or under the road.

- If there are dogs in the neighborhood, they will start barking because they hear and feel his presence.

- A strange breeze will move up the four roads at the same time towards the center, which forms his presence.

Of course, as a kid, I thought this was merely a scary ghost story in line with other stories I'd heard, like the grey ladies of death who wander the back roads or the devil dogs that herald death or indicate a road into the spirit world. After I grew up and encountered all of these beings, I found that they are not merely superstitions. They are stories about spirits of great power. Later in life, I had my first encounter with the Dark Rider at a crossroads in Virginia and found that every single element my mother described presented itself. Over time and work with the Dark Rider, as well as discussions with other folks who work with him, I have found him to be one of the most powerful and helpful of the traditional spirits of conjure. But I warn you that though he does not require you to sell your immortal soul to him, he does require integrity and a promise from you in exchange for the road openings he provides. There are many reasons why people go to this spirit, such as to learn a new skill, to open a road that seems closed, to gain wisdom about the right roads to take, or simply to hear his instructions with your inner ear.

When you encounter him, you will have no doubt that you are in the presence of great power. I share with you a powerful poem written by a dear friend after meeting the Dark Rider at a weekend conjure intensive I taught in Southern California in August 2001:

At three in the morning all that's solid, still, and unseen awakens. The secret dreams that sleep below the surface of the sunlit mind awaken. The shadows between trees, behind stones, and under beds awaken. The cemetery, small and innocuous under the noon sun, now at this sacred hour, appears vast and vivacious.

But we're not looking to mingle with bones or shadows tonight—we mean to summon something that never sleeps: a pitch black horse with coal for eyes, and a Rider that's even darker.

Night after night they ride through this old town, pounding the road in pursuit of the Dawn, but always a few hours behind it. Dark and his Rider perpetually journey in the Earth's shadow. Are they the Earth's shadow? The question throws a blanket of chill over my shoulders as me and my blessed family of seekers navigate the scrubby, red earth in near darkness—seeking a power spot.

It's a strange way to come to the crossroads—as a large and loving family. What's normally an eerie and lonely walk, in desperation sought—is now a giddy group outing. I've always said the crossroads are somewhere you shouldn't be, standing on the tracks of animals you hope not to meet, far enough into the wild that no one will hear you scream. I've said the approach should be lonely, hungry, humble, mostly naked, and armed with sincere strength of heart as well as something a little sharper. I'm not saying Spirit won't show up in your living room, I'm saying that effort is an excellent offering.

But we've brought shiny and intoxicating gifts that we hope will offset the short and crowded journey down past the fence's edge and not much further. We put down a red lantern—a traffic signal for the Rider to stop here and have a drink before continuing on his way. The sharp rumble as he revs his engine while idling at the light elicits nervous laughter from the group. Where's the horse?

The wind kicks up on the ridge and the rumbling spirit-engine becomes a deafening roar in my ears. Time to stack my small pennies and say my prayers . . . but it's a big blessing I'm seeking. I ain't going to ask for something small—I feel like asking for inconsequential gifts is how folks test the water. I don't test the Rider. He turns to me and winks at my tornado-powered lightning-struck barefoot-running okra-lickin creek-jumping southern-fried soul.

"You think pennies and a shot aren't right payment for a big healing like that? What if I think your healing ain't so big? What if to me it's just a small thing? Maybe to you it should be too. You think about that, remember it, and I'll see it done, sweet child. My sweet, gracious, dangerous little star—you are quite the blinding sight for dark eyes like mine."

—REN ZAPTOPEK, "PENNIES AT THE CROSSROADS"

Ren's deep wisdom and poetic power and her genuine encounter with the Dark Rider are apparent in this beautiful writing.

I will not provide all of the formula for meeting the Dark Rider in this book, but I will include some information on his power and some of the elements of encountering him. This is not a being to be trivialized. In fact, none of the beings I have introduced to you are trivial in any way. But I will provide a simple way to leave a petition for the Dark Rider's help that is powerful, respectful, and lacks the more subtle nuances and teachings you need for a full-force encounter.

To do this, you should go to the crossroads with a spirit worker who has a long-time relationship with the Dark Rider, like me. Ren's poem already provides some of the instruction I gave in my direct guidance to my conjure students.

A Simple Petition to the Dark Rider

Here is a simple but powerful rite to summon the Dark Rider:

1. Find a safe and secluded four-way crossroads. Unless you have an experienced crossroads-working conjurer, I recommend that you find a walking path in a park or somewhere you will not be in car traffic.

2. The best time to go to the crossroads is three a.m. on a Wednesday morning.

3. Have three new pennies or leap year-dated Mercury-head dimes and some rum or Crown Royal whiskey plus a small biodegradable paper cup with you.

4. Have two skeleton-type keys with you. Before taking these keys to the Dark Rider, you should wash them in pure water, anoint them in Florida Water cologne, and pray over them to be an instrument of God and his good spirits. For a few weeks before doing this working, you should carry the two keys in a pouch and let them clang against each together. In this way, they talk to each other and with your inner spirit.

5. Anoint yourself using the crowning technique with hyssop oil.

6. Knock at the center of the crossways three times, saying, "Dark Rider, I call to you in the name of the Maker (or Father, Son, and Holy Spirit) to open my good roads of fortune."

7. Wait until you feel a response in the wind. It is fine to use a discernment tool also.

8. Ask the Dark Rider to open your road (life, death, luck, or love) depending on your needs. Dig a small hole in the dirt (if you can), put one key in the hole for the Dark Rider, and cover it up, leaving this key in his hand.

9. Place your three coins on the ground in the center of the crossways with the heads pointing outward. Set your cup filled with liquor in the center of the triangle as an offering.

10. Thank him and knock on the ground three times again while saying, "Let this spirit door be closed, Dark Rider, until I call again." Feel the door close and his spirit go back into the other world. Then leave with your other key, knowing that you have a potent charm as a connection to the Dark Rider.

11. When in need related to your petition, wear your key in a red flannel bag on the right side of your body to lead you to the right doors in life.

This working will give you a safe introduction to this incredible spirit. May your key open good roads in your life and may your thresholds of blessings open to you.

Chapter 10

Working the Root

To work the root, you have to touch the power of the work as spirit to spirit.

—ORION FOXWOOD

It seems fitting to end by coming back to the root, which is the spirit or essence of creation itself. What makes the magic of southern conjure so powerful is that it moves us from our head into a place where the very core of our being touches the core of our work. This can be a challenge for many, because it makes you get true with who you are at a deep and profound level. I feel there are many reasons for this. The primary reason is that this type of work grew out of soulfulness and survived against seemingly insurmountable odds. In its survival, it seems to have been distilled down to basic and powerful truths that are accessible through direct techniques.

Tucked away in the practices are some very powerful state-
ments about working this form of conjure.

• You have to represent yourself to the spirit world to gain
  the fullest benefit of it.

• You need to make space for a consistent relationship with
  the spirit world, not just one based on desperation.

• There are many gateways into this relationship.

• Conjure is an act of co-creation and spiritual relationships
  based on reciprocity. Our own inner spirit requires attention and maintenance, like all aspects of us, and it is our
  primary gate.

• You have to consciously choose your spirit relationships
  and attend to them.

• The painful illusions of life and the futility of outworn patterns can be healed through relationships with both tides
  of life.

These are only a few of the teachings at the core of spirit
doctoring. As you do this work and expand upon it with your
own research and experience, the practices will reach out and
gift their precious gems to you. This is part of the distilla-
tion process that the spirits and practitioners of conjure have
undergone since its long journey started hundreds of years
ago. Before giving my final conjure teachings, I want to review
what I have advised you, as a potential spirit worker, to do up
to this point:

• Give respect to the origins of spirit work as a product of
  suffering, sorrow, and fortitude.

- Get to know your own inner spirit and the ways it has been influenced by your ethnic, cultural, and generational paradoxes and opportunities.

- Preserve the folk teachings of your family and culture because they may have great power to offer.

- Develop a routine for contacting God and cleansing your spirit inwardly and outwardly as a way of fostering that relationship.

- Choose the spirit forces (embodied and other) with discernment and discretion.

- Work with ancestral spirits as your closest next of kin in the invisible world.

- Work with threshold states and gateways to the inner world often so that you never lessen the potential of your relationship with it.

- Enjoy the beauty of life by extending your life across the full spectrum of the spirit tides, giving attention to them as the blessings of divinity.

These teachings are deep, old, and time-honored, but they are not to be treated as *the* conjure or any other form of false orthodoxy. They are to stimulate your interest and inspire you to work further on knowing the root within yourself and in all things.

Now, let's have some final fun and work with some plant roots that are sacred among the root workers. We'll use a time-honored formula for working the root, and we'll work with an old form of making a spirit bag, or mojo. This book will not provide an extensive list of roots to be used for conjure, as there are many other fine books on the subject. What it does provide, which other books often do not contain, is techniques for tapping in to and working with the spirit powers of the botanical root and the root powers in other material used in conjure.

Summoning Forth the Spirit

Workers use many plant roots in this work, and each has its own unique and incredible spirit and power. However, there is some very powerful guidance for summoning forth the power and the spirit in the root. As always, there are many insights that you can gain about how this works if you look at the inferences in the formula below. Remember that all of the items you work with in conjure have spirits in them and that mere intent does not stir the spirit and its power to work for you. You have to draw forth the spirit within it and treat it as a person, not a thing. The formula below is for plant roots, but it can be applied in work with any powerful force you are using, such as a stone, bone, teeth, herb part, or fetish. Here is the formula, which you can use to serve your work:

- **Tapping:** This is the technique I referred to as knocking or tapping at the door to spirit. It is simply gently tapping three times on the root stating, "Awaken unto life."

- **Honoring:** This involves bringing the root to your mouth close enough that your breath can touch it while saying, "I honor you (insert name of root)."

- **Summoning Power:** This involves saying to the root, "Remember your power." It calls the spirit within the root back to the surface world because they often retreat deeper into themselves during disrespectful forms of growing and harvesting. Now say, "Release your power to (whatever you are summoning out since many roots do many different actions)."

- **Feeding:** This involves practices to strengthen and feed the power of the spirit in the root, such as soaking it in rum or whiskey (or sprinkling rum or whiskey on it for herb parts), setting it in a triangle of lit white vigil candles to feed it fire, or even sprinkling it with coffee to fire it up.

- **Dressing:** This involves anointing the root after it has been fed and dried if liquid feeding was provided. I usually use some form of power oil or olive oil.

- **Working:** This involves putting the root in a red flannel bag and carrying it to work its power for your goal.

- **Feeding More:** As you work a root, it might grow weak or hungry. Simply take it out and feed it again or leave it in its pouch and sprinkle it with rum, feed with the triangle of fire described earlier, and then re-dress either the root or the bag.

When you are not working with your root, either give it back to the earth or put it to bed to be worked at another time. Putting it to bed is as simple as thanking it for its work and letting it know it can rest, but you will call upon its spirit again. Then put it in a box or a special place for it to sleep. When you are ready to work with it again just repeat the formula I gave you above. Now, let's work with a specific root—the one most known to root workers these days and most discussed in the media—known as High John the Conqueror, which I also know as Good Johnny Root.

Working the High John the Conqueror Root

There is some conjecture about when and how the fame of this root started. Some say that it was not even the currently famed root (*Ipomoea jalap*, related to the morning glory and sweet potato). Regardless, this root has gained a reputation, and I have found that a powerful spirit lives in it and offers great power to the worker. It has many reputed uses, such as winning court cases, enhancing male sexual potency, and increasing gambling luck, but is never taken internally. My teachers referred to it as the king of the conjure roots and a power root that can increase the power of whatever it is added to. According to the lore, the spirit that lives in this root origi-nated in Africa. It used to live in another root and came over to our country swimming in the sweat of the slaves. The spirit in the root, which I will refer to as John, is the liberator of the oppressed and embodies the power of the root worker as I know it. John comes to break the chains of domination, give an upper hand to the downtrodden, grant liberation from oppression, and give power to the powerless. This root is not like most roots used in magic—it is not just a virtue or energy. It is a home for a particular allied spirit much like mandrake (*Mandragora officinarum*), which in European witchcraft is a home for a powerful spirit and is fed, dressed, and cared for as a familiar spirit. One does not need a lot of High John roots to work with, because each one has to be treated as a powerful spirit, unless you are working with one for power, one for sex, one for legal work, and so on. Personally, I do not think that multiple roots are necessary when one root can do all of these powers if asked to.

I was taught that there are male and female roots. Honestly, all of them feel like a male power to me, but I do not think the root cares about this. The lore is that if they are pointed on the ends and phallic or tubular shaped, they are boys. If they are round or vaginal shaped, they are girls. My teachers said that both shapes have the same powerful spirit, except they work in historically American-based gender-expressive ways as in how men versus women stereotypically behave. Of course we know those labels are culture-based and do not reflect reality. But, given the context that the lore was provided to me, here are the gender symbolic attributes of these roots:

- **Male roots** are for winning court cases, gaining physical strength, overcoming obstacles, male sexual potency, and dominating any situation.

- **Female roots** are for general magnetism and attraction, intrigue, female potency, and drawing the attention of powerful people to you.

For a general power spirit bag, I have found that you can use both together. If you choose this route (or root), then each will have to be taken through the formula for summoning the spirit given above.

There are a few more added instructions when working with these roots. I find that it is useful to either procure them in person or work through a root worker who knows you and your needs well. Their potency is enhanced when the human has a connection to them. If you are choosing your root(s), it can be useful to use one of the discernment tools. This allows you and the spirit of the root to choose each other. When you bring the root or roots home, use the formula I gave you. However, when you feed the root, keep the rum or whiskey that you feed or soak the root in because it also has power. You can take this brown tobacco-smelling liquid and use it to either dress the root when you wear it out (though this increases the alcohol smell on you); anoint the doorframe of your front door to bring in luck and to protect you; or sprinkle it throughout your home to lay a floor of power, protection, and general good luck. It can also be mixed with Hoyt's cologne and sprinkled in your money pot.

Other Roots Plus One Powerful Seed

Workers vary in their favorite roots. I consider all of them together to be like a root worker's first-aid kit. What I am providing for you below is a list of some of my favorite roots. Apply the previous formula to the use of each of these roots, except where stated.

Other John Roots

There are two other John roots I work with: Chewing John (*Alpinia galangal*), also known as Low or Little John, is edible and used for winning court cases and drawing money. Virginia John (*Trillium grandiflorum*), also known as Dixie John and Rattlesnake root, is used to ward off the bite of enemies, increase luck at gambling, and increase the sexual attractiveness of the wearer.

Archangel Root

This is the root of the angelica plant (*Angelica archangelica*) and is used to enhance High John, as an offering or house for the Archangel Michael for protection and truth spells, or tied to the end of a red string and used as a pendulum because it tells the truth. It can also be burned as an incense to clear a home or other items of bad energy and wicked spiritual forces. It also attracts powerful protective forces to women and children.

Master Root

This root (*Imperatoria ostruthium*) will enhance the power of a root worker. It both enhances the range and accuracy of the worker's spirit senses and protects the worker from malevolent influences. You can enhance its power by using High John oil or the whiskey or rum used to feed High John to feed or dress the Master Root.

Peony Root

Interestingly, this root (*Paeonia officinalis*) was called "piney root" by my mother and others I learned from in Virginia. It was not until I moved to Maryland that I learned it was called "peony root" by the rest of the world. This feminine root is carried to promote healing, a shift from bad to good luck, and for general protection of love-related relationships, such as parenting, friendship, and romance.

Rattlesnake Root (Gentian)

This root (*Gentiana catesbaei*) is used to ward off enemies and to draw those who truly care about you. In my conjure teachings, Grandfather Rattlesnake is the power of God that descends from the heavens and protects you by striking enemies, but he gives intuitive warning. He also gives power, virility to men, and can (like many snake roots) be used to draw sex and sometimes love.

Orris Root

This root (*Iris florentina*) is also known as iris or Queen Root and is a very feminine root that enhances a woman's sexual attraction. I have heard of it being used by men who love men to attract loving partners. Like peony, she is a root for lovers and marriages but has a special power for attracting men to women or gay or bisexual men. I have heard it is powerful for a discernment pendulum, specifically for romance.

❖ ❖ ❖

This ends my introduction to the conjurer's first-aid kit. I have one more botanical that I recommend as an across-the-board powerful companion in root work—a seed called Grains of Paradise, also known as Guinea Peppers.

Grains of Paradise

The Grains of Paradise (*Aframonum melegueta*) are very small seeds with a lot of power. They can be used to bring or get rid of an influence. Three seeds can be placed into the worker's mouth while he or she prays to be rid of an influence, and they are spit out at a crossroads or a river running away from the worker. If you have something you are working to make happen, pray with three seeds in your mouth, and then chew and swallow them. In legal cases, Grains of Paradise are powerful when held in the space between the cheek and the gums until the case is won during trial. This was one of Marie Laveau's favorite workings.

❖ ❖ ❖

These roots and seeds can be used in conjunction with other curios, such as minerals, herbs, teeth, bones, claws, and medallions to form a spirit bag, also known as a mojo or lucky hand. Though there are many formulas for making these living prayers, I will provide you with an old-style one that I was taught. It has proven power.

Making a Spirit Bag

A spirit bag is a bag of spiritual forces that have been empowered and awakened to strengthen the power of the wearer. They are a very powerful force when they are created in a powerful way. Every aspect of the bag—the bag, its strings, the lips of the bag, and its contents—comes together as one powerful spirit being working for its wearer. There should be only an odd number of ingredients—usually no more than nine or possibly eleven—brought together in a red flannel bag. This bag is traditionally made from the sweat-covered cloth of a flannel shirt, also known as a working man's shirt sewed or closed with the string from feed or seed bags. These bags are living spirits in and of themselves and are not a quick project to assemble if they are to have power. Here is the old-style formula that I learned:

1. Identify the kind of goal you wish to achieve, as this is both the spirit and the voice of the spirit bag.

2. Bring together all of the items for the bag, being sure to have an odd-numbered mix of botanicals, minerals, animal parts (teeth, claws, bones, etc.), and metals.

3. Cleanse each one of them using any of the techniques provided.

4. Cleanse the red flannel bag, as it is the lung of the prayer bag.

5. Ask God or the Maker to grant you the power for this work. I usually do this by reaching my hands heavenward and asking for the power and for God to work through me.

6. Awaken each one of the items by tapping, honoring, awakening, and summoning their powers.

7. Feed each one with any of the ways I have shared with you.

8. Place each one into the bag.

9. After all of them are in the bag, take three wooden matches. Light them one by one, quickly put the lit match into the mouth of the pouch, and pull it out so

fast that the match goes out, leaving the energy of the flame within the bag without catching it on fire. This gives more light to the bag.

10. Once everything is in the bag, close it with three knots. Take a power oil such as High John or olive oil and anoint the whole bag with an "X" starting from the left top side and drawing down toward the bottom right, then from the right top side drawing toward the left bottom to complete the "X." Anoint all the way around the edges of the bag. Repeat these steps on the other side of the bag. This pulls the power together into one spirit. When you are finished, reach to God and draw power down like a lightning bolt to the center of the "X" signs on the two sides of the bag to give it more power.

11. Now you are ready to wear this bag for your wellbeing. If it is to control a situation, put it on the right side of the body. If it is to attract, put it on the left.

12. From time to time, feed the bag with some drops of rum, whiskey, or coffee to keep it alive. When it is done, put it to sleep like you did with the High John root.

❖ ❖ ❖

May these conjure practices bring you success and healthy power in your work. May the four roads of spirit lay open before you . . .

Afterword

I can only lead you do the door of spirit. Only you can open it and enter. May blessings abound as you walk the spirit road.

—ORION FOXWOOD AND JOHNNIE ROOSTER

As you can see, American southern conjure is a path unto itself. The challenges related to this path are that it requires the student to walk the same path that the workers before have walked. This path is one of spiritual sovereignty in the face of oppression and adversity. It is one that demands the seeker look at his or her own spirit to access its power. It is indeed a soulful path of magic and spirit. It is a path of truth!

I have walked three major magical roads in my life: old-style traditional witchcraft, Faery Seership, and conjure. All three have demanded that I look into different components of my being. All three have given me back to myself in ways that would require a whole other book to explain. Conjure has taught me why the African slaves could not lose their spirit, even in the face of ungodly and unspeakable horrors. It has taught me how no force in this world can diminish our spirit, no matter what it may appear or feel like. Conjure is a path that requires us to be real and authentic at the very core of who we are and who we wish to be.

It is indeed with raised head and bended knee that I thank the African people who crossed the ocean by the forces of slavery and never, ever lost their spirit. It is with astounding gratitude and unbending loyalty that I serve you and all those persons who formed the very foundations of our country by paving roads to the future with their very lives. I thank the many people, cultures, and ethnic groups, the many religions and spiritual traditions and practices that inform the corpus of conjure.

I end this book with a quote from Zora Neale Hurston's 1942 classic, *Dust Tracks on a Road*: "People can be slave-ships in shoes." We can be enslaved to our ancestral paradoxes, our inherited patterns, or our accumulated past, but we can be liberated and these chains can be severed. May we not become slaves to our past. May we embody the hopes of our ancestors while not being the curse of our past. May we doctor our root in a way that grows a future that is whole, clean, healed, and prosperous. We are not doomed by the past; we are informed by it. May you bring the candle spirit to the crossroads of your becoming and liberate your being.

May this book liberate all who read it from the shackles of inner slavery and free the indwelling spirit to become the image that God saw when your creation was inspired into becoming *you!*

Recommended Reading

I recommend several fine books for insight and information on the magical practices of the American South, Appalachia, and the African-American culture. Known under various names—conjure, root doctoring, and hoodoo—elements of all three of these traditions have influenced how I practice and the understanding of what I do from a historical and cultural viewpoint. Though nearly all of the information I have provided here came from oral traditions shared with me by family members, neighbors, and other teachers and direct-spirit sources, I have found the following books to be very useful.

Alvarado, Denise. *The Voodoo Hoodoo Spellbook*. San Francisco, CA: Weiser Books, 2011.

Anderson, Jeffrey E. *Conjure in African American Society*. Baton Rouge, LA: Louisiana University Press, 2005.

——— *Hoodoo, Voodoo and Conjure: A Handbook*. Westport, CT: Greenwood Press, 2008.

Berry, Jason. *The Spirit of Blackhawk: The Mystery of Africans and Indians*. Jackson, MS: University Press of Mississippi, 1995.

Casas, Starr. *BlackHawk: Working with His Spirit*. Self-Published (www.oldstyleconjure.com), 2010.

———— *Old Style Spiritual Cleansing: A Guide to Opening the Way.* Self-Published (OldStyleConjure.com), 2010.

Cavender, Anthony. *Folk Medicine in Southern Appalachia.* Chapel Hill, NC: The University of North Carolina Press, 2003.

Chireau, Yvonne P. *Black Magic: Religion and the African American Conjuring Tradition.* Berkeley, CA: University of California Press, 2003.

Filan, Kenaz. *The New Orleans Voodoo Handbook.* Rochester, VT: Destiny Books, 2011.

Gamache, Henri. *The Master Book of Candle Burning.* Plainview, NY: Original Publications, 1998.

Hurston, Zora Neale. *Mules and Men.* New York: Harper and Row Publishers, 1935

———— *The Sanctified Church: The Folklore Writings of Zora Neale Hurston.* Berkeley, CA: Turtle Island Foundation, 1981.

Hyatt, Harry M. *Folklore from Adams County Illinois.* Memoirs of the Alma Egan Hyatt Foundation, 1935.

Long-Morrow, Carolyn. *A New Orleans Voudou Priestess: The Legend and Reality of Marie Laveau.* Gainesville, FL: University Press of Florida, 2006.

Malborough, Ray. *Hoodoo Mysteries: Folk Magic, Mysticism and Rituals.* St. Paul, MN: Llewellyn Publications, 2003.

Pinckney, Roger. *Blue Roots: African-American Folk Magic of the Gullah People.* St. Paul, MN: Llewellyn Publications, 1998.

Puckett, Newbell Niles. *Folk Beliefs of the Southern Negro.* Kessinger Publishing's Rare Reprints (originally published 1925).

Raboteau, Albert J. *Slave Religion: The "Invisible Institution" in the Antebellum South.* New York: Oxford University Press, 1980.

Ward, Martha. *Voodoo Queen: The Spirited Lives of Marie Laveau.* Jackson, MS: University Press of Mississippi, 2004.

Wiggington, Eliot, ed. *Foxfire (11 Volumes on Southern Appalachian Culture and Practices).* The Foxfire Foundation at *www.foxfire.org.*

Yronwode, Catherine. *Hoodoo Herb and Root Magic: A Materia Magica of African-American Conjure.* Forestville, CA: Lucky Mojo Curio Company, 2002.

Resources

I am a part of a collaborative effort of five conjurers, hoodoo and root workers who have come together to preserve and promote the healing and helping benefits of these practices. The collaborative is called Conjure Crossroads, and it hosts an annual Folk Magic Festival and other events providing hands-on teaching and training in conjure work. These events are unique and high quality, reflecting the heart and soul of conjure.

Information and other resources provided by its members can be found at *www.conjurecrossroads.com* and *www.folkmagicfestival.com.*

Lucky Mojo Curio Company founded by Catherine Yronwode is one of the largest purveyors of hoodoo, conjure, and root-work information and materials in the world. It is a major resource and can be accessed through *www.luckymojo.com.*

Priestess Miriam of the Voodoo Spiritual Temple in New Orleans is a deeply loved and respected Voodoo Mambo and educational resource on the syncretic nature and sacred practices of American Voodoo. Her temple and educational center offer an invaluable resource. More information on Priestess Miriam and her temple can be found at *www.voodoospiritualtemple.org.*

When visiting New Orleans, one of the most resourceful and informed historians, tour guides, and New Orleans Voodoo Mambos you will find is Mary Milan, also known as Bloody Mary of Bloody Mary's Tours. For information on Mary and her tours, see *www.bloodymarystours.com*.

About the Author

Orion Foxwood is a conjurer in the American southern folk tradition, a traditional witch, and a Faery Seer. He is the founder of Foxwood Temple of the Old Religion in Maryland and the House of Brigh Faery Seership Institute, and a co-founder of Conjure Crossroads and the annual Folk Magic Festival held in New Orleans. For over 25 years he has lectured extensively and been a media and public presence on Southern Conjure, witchcraft, folk magic and Faery practices, and other magical and spiritual subjects. He is the author of two books, *The Faery Teachings* and *The Tree of Enchantment*; DVDs *Introduction to Faery Seership*, *Introduction to Southern Conjure*, and *Orion: On the Goddess*; and a collaborative CD project with RJ Stewart, *Faery Seership*. He was born and raised in the Shenandoah Valley in Virginia. Visit him online at: *www.orionfoxwood.com.*

To Our Readers